Social Issues
in Literature

Depression in
J.D. Salinger's
The Catcher in the Rye

Other Books in the Social Issues in Literature Series:

Social Issues
in Literature

Depression in J.D. Salinger's *The Catcher in the Rye*

Dedria Bryfonski, Book Editor

GREENHAVEN PRESS
A part of Gale, Cengage Learning

GALE
CENGAGE Learning

Detroit • New York • San Francisco • New Haven, Conn • Waterville, Maine • London

Christine Nasso, *Publisher*
Elizabeth Des Chenes, *Managing Editor*

© 2009 Greenhaven Press, a part of Gale, Cengage Learning

Gale and Greenhaven Press are registered trademarks used herein under license.

For more information, contact:
Greenhaven Press
27500 Drake Rd.
Farmington Hills, MI 48331-3535
Or you can visit our Internet site at gale.cengage.com

For product information and technology assistance, contact us at

Gale Customer Support, 1-800-877-4253
For permission to use material from this text or product, submit all requests online at
www.cengage.com/permissions

Further permissions questions can be emailed to permissionrequest@cengage.com

Articles in Greenhaven Press anthologies are often edited for length to meet page requirements. In addition, original titles of these works are changed to clearly present the main thesis and to explicitly indicate the author's opinion. Every effort is made to ensure that Greenhaven Press accurately reflects the original intent of the authors. Every effort has been made to trace the owners of copyrighted material.

Cover photograph reproduced by permission of © Bettmann/CORBIS.

LIBRARY OF CONGRESS CATALOGING-IN-PUBLICATION DATA

Depression in J.D. Salinger's The catcher in the rye / Dedria Bryfonski, book editor.
   p. cm. -- (Social issues in literature)
   Includes bibliographical references and index.
   ISBN-13: 978-0-7377-4256-5 (hbk.)
   ISBN-13: 978-0-7377-4257-2 (pbk.)
   1. Salinger, J. D. (Jerome David), 1919- Catcher in the rye--Juvenile literature.
2. Depression, Mental, in literature--Juvenile literature. 3. Salinger, J. D. (Jerome David), 1919--Characters--Holden Caulfield--Juvenile literature. 4. Caulfield, Holden (Fictitious character)--Juvenile literature. 5. Depression, Mental--Juvenile literature. 6. Depression in adolescence--Juvenile literature. I. Bryfonski, Dedria.
   PS3537.A426C326 2009
   813'.54--dc22

                                   2008033613

Printed in the United States of America
2 3 4 5 6   18 17 16 15 14

Contents

Chapter 1: The Background of J.D. Salinger

Warren French

The publication of *The Catcher in the Rye* in 1951 was the watershed event of Salinger's early career. He had been working on versions of "the Holden Caulfield story" for a decade, introducing characters by that name into his short stories and working on a draft of a novel. Salinger's experiences in World War II, however, caused him to re-shape Holden into the more complex character that can be seen in *The Catcher in the Rye.*

David L. Stevenson

Although Salinger's works are not strictly autobiographical, he uses events and settings from his life throughout his fiction, as well as a technique referred to as the *New Yorker* writer.

Chapter 2: *The Catcher in the Rye* and Depression

Harrison Smith

Holden Caulfield despairs at the phoniness he sees around him and is acutely drawn to beauty and innocence. Salinger's genius in *The Catcher in the Rye* is in the way in which he uses colloquial language to capture the emotions of a troubled adolescent.

Chapter 3: Contemporary Perspectives on Depression

Introduction

With his character of Holden Caulfield, J.D. Salinger struck a chord with millions of young readers who felt he was putting into words their deepest, unarticulated feelings. All of a sudden there was a spokesman for teenage angst, whether the author welcomed the role or not. Reviewing the novel for the *Nation* in 1951, critic Ernest Jones terms *The Catcher in the Rye* "a case history of all of us."

Looking at Salinger's earlier career, it would have been hard to predict the overwhelming success of his only novel, which has sold approximately 65 million copies and continues to sell about 250,000 copies a year. Salinger began writing when he was fifteen and determined at an early age to become a professional writer. While he had some successes and was published in the leading "slicks" (magazines so termed because of their glossy covers) of the day, his early works are generally considered minor pieces. According to the critic Arthur Mizener ("The Love Song of J.D. Salinger"):

> Salinger did not burst on the world with these powers of observation and this sense of experience fully developed. He had, in fact, rather more trouble than most writers in discovering his own way of feeling and the best mode of expression for it. His first published stories, which appeared mainly in the *Saturday Evening Post* and *Collier's* in the early forties, will quickly destroy any romantic notions one may have had about the value of the unpublished stories he wrote even earlier.... The first published stories deal, in a mechanical and overingenious way, with the superficial interests of magazine readers of the time.

It took a major event in world history and in Salinger's life—World War II—to provide experiences that would add an emotional intensity to his writing that had not been present before. Most critics divide Salinger's career into two parts—a prewar period, comprising minor short stories written for popular magazines, and a period dating from the end of World War II until he ceased publishing in 1965, which is characterized by fiction that is much more complex, and which is dominated by a concern with the theme of madness. World War II may have had a deleterious effect on Salinger the man—he suffered a nervous breakdown during the war—but it had a positive effect on Salinger the writer, as he almost certainly used his own psychic struggles to add a new depth and maturity to his work.

Salinger's career, like that of many other young men of the time, was interrupted and changed by the bombing of Pearl Harbor. Previously turned down for active service because of a minor heart condition, Salinger was drafted when classifications were redefined following the attack on Pearl Harbor. He was trained as a member of the Officers, First Sergeants, and Instructors School of the Signal Corps and eventually became a member of the Fourth Infantry Division, where he was trained in counterintelligence. Salinger was among those who landed on Utah Beach in Normandy on D-Day. In the weeks after D-Day, Salinger was part of the Allied troops conducting interrogation work in a war zone. In a letter to Whit Burnett, editor of *Story* magazine, Salinger alluded to the unspeakable horrors he had seen. Burnett's biographer Paul Alexander describes that letter:

> For the better part of the month, Salinger had been in a war zone where, as he witnessed mass death and destruction, he knew he, too, could be killed at any moment. As a result, the light-hearted, jovial tone he had affected in many of his past letters was gone, replaced by a solemnity usually foreign to Salinger. In fact, in his letter, Salinger told Burnett he simply could not describe the events of the last three or four weeks. What he had witnessed was too horrendous to put into words.

Unfortunately, this was just the beginning of fighting for the Fourth Division, which would have eleven months of combat in Europe, suffering some two thousand casualties a month.

These experiences took their toll on Salinger. In the spring of 1945, he was admitted to a hospital in Nuremberg, Germany, suffering from what was then termed battle fatigue, and what would today probably be termed post-traumatic stress disorder. His treatment was successful to the extent that he was sent back to his duties a few weeks later and that he received an honorable, rather than a psychiatric, discharge from the army.

According to his daughter, Margaret, however, his wartime experiences remained a significant part of Salinger's life. As she relates in *Dream Catcher: A Memoir,*

> While the war was often in the foreground of our family life, it was *always* in the background. It was the point of reference that defined everything else in relation to it. When Daddy took pleasure at being warm and dry and cozy by the fire, it was the pleasure of a man who has been truly cold and wet and miserable in his life. . . .

> The constant presence of the war, as something not really over, pervaded the years I lived at home. Even as a teenager, when I came home for a visit and he was bugging me about *some*thing, the way parents of teenagers seem to do, I said graciously, "Dad, will you quit interrogating me already!" He said, "I can't help it, that's what I am." Not in the past tense, but in the present as though he were still in counterintelligence uniform, interrogating prisoners. "That's what I am."

According to the National Institute of Mental Health, post-traumatic stress disorder (PTSD) is "an anxiety disorder that can develop after exposure to a terrifying event or ordeal in which grave physical harm occurred or was threatened." People suffering from PTSD sometimes revisit their trauma through vivid memories and flashbacks. Symptoms of PTSD include heightened anxiety, depression, an exaggerated vigilance, and a sense of emotional detachment.

It is impossible to know which of these symptoms led to Salinger's hospitalization in Nuremberg. We can speculate that by experiencing psychological distress firsthand, Salinger was able to transfer such feelings to his characters, imbuing them with a depth that was not present in his pre-war work. A notable example is Sergeant X in "For Esmé—with Love and Squalor." Sergeant X shares so many details in common with Salinger that the short story is considered autobiographical. Salinger writes that the sergeant "is a young man who had not come through the war with all his faculties intact."

Leslie Fiedler dated this short story, published in 1950, as the beginning of Salinger's mature writing period, also marking the beginning of his preoccupation with madness as a theme. Fiedler wrote in "Up from Adolescence":

> I am referring, of course, to Salinger's presentation of madness as the chief temptation of modern life, especially for the intelligent young, and his conviction that, consequently, the chief heroism possible to us now is the rejection of madness, the decision to be sane. What suicide was for the young Werther [hero of *The Sorrows of Young Werther* by Johann Wolfgang von Goethe] or running away from home for Huck Finn [hero of *The Adventures of Huckleberry Finn* by Mark Twain], the "nervous breakdown," Salinger urges us to believe, is for the sensitive adolescent of our time.

Depression and madness are certainly major themes of *The Catcher in the Rye*, and part of the power of the narrative emerges from the way Salinger captures the angst of a sensitive teenager driven into mental illness. What causes Holden Caulfield's depression and descent into madness is the subject of debate in the essays that follow. What is clear, however, is that many of the symptoms Holden displays in the course of the novel mirror the classic symptoms of post-traumatic stress disorder.

The death of his younger brother, Allie, was a traumatic event in Holden Caulfield's life and is perhaps at the root of the depression he battles in the novel. The death of a sibling can trigger post-traumatic stress disorder, and one of its symptoms is the type of memory he evokes of breaking all the windows in the garage the night Allie died, then trying to break all the windows in the station wagon. Another symptom of PTSD is present in the episode with the prostitute, where Holden says, "I felt more depressed than sexy, if you want to know the truth." And perhaps the most compelling example occurs as Holden is walking up Fifth Avenue:

> Then, all of a sudden, something very spooky started happening. Every time I came to the end of a block and stepped off the goddam curb, I had this feeling that I'd never get to the other side of the street. I thought I'd just go down, down, down, and nobody'd ever see me again. Boy, did it scare me. You can't imagine. I started sweating like a bastard—my whole shirt and underwear and everything.

The hyperalertness and anxiety in this episode are classic examples of PTSD. Salinger began writing versions of *The Catcher in the Rye* as early as 1941, but it was not until 1949 that he began revising and creating the final work. Some of the most powerful scenes in the book were created after World War II by a man who had personal experience with the effects of extreme stress in his own life.

In the essays that follow, critics detail the symptoms of madness and depression that Salinger brings alive in Holden Caulfield. Chapter 3 presents contemporary perspectives on adolescent depression, including suggestions for coping with it. While critics disagree about the cause of Holden Caulfield's depression, no one can dispute the impact on American culture of J.D. Salinger's portrait of a troubled youth.

Chronology

1919
Jerome David Salinger is born on January 1 in New York City, the second child and only son of Sol and Miriam Jillich Salinger.

1932
Salinger's family moves to an apartment on the corner of Park Avenue and East 91st Street, and Salinger is enrolled in McBurney School in Manhattan.

1934–1936
Salinger attends Valley Forge Military Academy, where he serves as literary editor of *Crossed Sabres*, the school yearbook, and begins writing short stories.

1937–1938
Salinger visits Vienna and Poland to learn about his father's ham and cheese importing business.

1938–1939
Salinger attends Ursinus College in Pennsylvania, where he writes a column titled "Skipped Diploma" for the college newspaper.

1939
Salinger attends Whit Burnett's short story writing class at Columbia University.

1940
"The Young Folks" is published in Whit Burnett's *Story* magazine. Salinger is paid twenty-five dollars. "Go See Eddie" is published in the *University of Kansas City Review* after being rejected by *Esquire*.

1941

"The Hang of It" is published in *Collier's* and "The Heart of a Broken Story" in *Esquire*. Salinger sells his first story about Holden Caulfield to the *New Yorker*, but because of World War II, publication is delayed until 1946. Following the bombing of Pearl Harbor, Salinger volunteers for the draft but is rejected because of a mild heart condition. He dates Oona O'Neill, daughter of playwright Eugene O'Neill. She breaks off the relationship to date Charlie Chaplin, whom she eventually marries.

1942

"The Long Debut of Lois Taggett" is published in *Story* and "Personal Notes of an Infantryman" in *Collier's*. Salinger is reclassified as 1-A and drafted into the U.S. Army. He attends Officers, First Sergeants, and Instructors School of Signal Corps.

1943

"The Varioni Brothers" is published in the *Saturday Evening Post*. Salinger is transferred to the Army Counter-Intelligence Corps with the rank of staff sergeant.

1944

"Last Day of the Last Furlough" and two other Salinger stories are published in the *Saturday Evening Post*. Salinger lands on Utah Beach on D-Day and participates in five campaigns in Europe. He meets Ernest Hemingway at the Ritz Hotel in Paris. Salinger shows Hemingway "The Last Day of the Last Furlough," which Hemingway says he likes. With his proficiency in French and German, Salinger is assigned to interrogate prisoners of war. He is among the first to enter a liberated concentration camp.

1945

Salinger is hospitalized in Nuremberg, Germany, for a psychiatric condition. He meets and marries a woman named Sylvia. Most biographers believe Sylvia was a French doctor; however,

Salinger's daughter writes that Sylvia was a "low level official of the Nazi party." Salinger is honorably discharged from the army. "Elaine" is published in *Story*, "This Sandwich Has No Mayonnaise" in *Esquire*, "A Boy in France" in the *Saturday Evening Post*. "I'm Crazy," the first published story to use material included in *The Catcher in the Rye*, is published in *Collier's*.

1946

"Slight Rebellion Off Madison," another forerunner of *The Catcher in the Rye*, is published in the *New Yorker*. A ninety-page novelette about Holden Caulfield is accepted for publication but withdrawn by Salinger. Salinger writes to a friend that his wife has decided to divorce him.

1947

"A Young Girl in 1941 with No Waist at All" is published in *Mademoiselle*, and "The Inverted Forest" is published in *Cosmopolitan*. Salinger moves to Westport, Connecticut.

1948

Salinger begins a long, exclusive relationship with the *New Yorker* upon the publication of "A Perfect Day for Bananafish," the first story about Seymour Glass. "Uncle Wiggily in Connecticut" is also published in the *New Yorker*. "A Girl I Knew," published in *Good Housekeeping*, is selected for *Best American Short Stories of 1949*. Salinger resumes work on the Holden Caulfield novel.

1950

"For Esmé—with Love and Squalor" is published in the *New Yorker*. *My Foolish Heart*, a film version of "Uncle Wiggily in Connecticut," is released by Samuel Goldwyn Studio. Early in the 1950s Salinger begins studying Advaita Vendanta under Swami Nikhilananda.

1951

The Catcher in the Rye is published on July 16. "Pretty Mouth and Green My Eyes" is published in the *New Yorker.*

1953

Salinger moves to Cornish, New Hampshire. He meets Claire Douglas, a 19-year-old Radcliffe College student, in Manchester, Vermont. "Teddy" is published in the *New Yorker. Nine Stories* is published on April 6.

1955

Salinger and Claire Douglas are married on February 17. "Franny" and "Raise High the Roof Beam, Carpenters" are published in the *New Yorker.* A daughter, Margaret Ann, is born to J.D. and Claire Salinger on December 10.

1957

"Zooey" is published in the *New Yorker.*

1959

"Seymour: An Introduction" is published in the *New Yorker.*

1960

A son, Matthew, is born to J.D. and Claire Salinger on February 13.

1961

Franny and Zooey is published on September 14.

1963

Raise High the Roof Beam, Carpenters and Seymour: An Introduction is published on January 28.

1965

Salinger's last work of fiction to be published, "Hapworth 16, 1924," is published in the *New Yorker.*

1967

Claire Salinger is granted a divorce from J.D. Salinger at Newport, New Hampshire, in November.

1972

Salinger begins a relationship with Joyce Maynard, an eighteen-year-old Yale student who gained instant celebrity when her article "An 18-Year-Old Looks Back on Life" appeared in the *New York Times Magazine*. Maynard moves in with Salinger for about ten months.

1986

Salinger is granted an injunction against the publication of an unauthorized biography by British writer Ian Hamilton that quotes from his letters.

1988

Ian Hamilton's biography of Salinger, rewritten to exclude quotations from his letters, is published as *In Search of J.D. Salinger*. About this time, Salinger marries Colleen O'Neill, who is forty years younger than him.

1999

Joyce Maynard publishes a memoir, *At Home in the World*, in which she describes her relationship with Salinger. She also puts his letters up for auction. They are purchased by software developer Peter Norton and returned to Salinger.

2000

Salinger's daughter, Margaret, publishes *Dream Catcher: A Memoir*.

The Background of J.D. Salinger

The Life of J.D. Salinger

Warren French

Warren French, Honorary Professor at the University of Wales, Swansea, has written a number of books on American writers. His book J.D. Salinger, Revisited is generally considered to be the most authoritative biography on the reclusive author.

According to Warren French, The Catcher in the Rye is not autobiographical, although Salinger did say in a rare interview that there is a "good deal" of himself in Holden Caulfield. In the following selection, French writes that Holden Caulfield inhabits the same world that Salinger grew up in—alternately living in an upper-middle-class Manhattan neighborhood and attending private schools. Salinger began writing in high school, and he continued to write short stories during and after college and throughout his service in World War II. He worked on various drafts of his only novel, The Catcher in the Rye, for a decade. Although it was published to generally favorable reviews, French states that no one anticipated on its publication that it would become a classic.

Born in New York City, Jerome David Salinger was the younger of two children and the only son born to Sol and Miriam Jillich Salinger. His father was a prosperous meat and cheese importer. The family lived in the fashionable apartment district of upper Manhattan, moving several times before fall 1932, when they settled in an apartment at the corner of Park Avenue and East Ninety-first Street, near the Metropolitan Museum of Art and Central Park—the area where Holden Caulfield's family also lives. At this time Salinger, who had been attending public schools, was enrolled at the fashionable and respected McBurney School in Manhattan. His

Warren French, *Dictionary of Literary Biography*. Farmington Hills, MI: The Gale Group, 1996. Reproduced by permission of Gale, a part of Cengage Learning.

grades there were below average, and in September 1934 he was sent to Valley Forge Military Academy in Pennsylvania. There he acted in school plays, edited the 1935–1936 class yearbook, and even wrote the lyrics for a quite conventional class song. He also began writing short stories.

None of the stories Salinger wrote at Valley Forge is known to survive, nor are there any from the three years immediately following his graduation in 1936. During that time he drifted. He spent late 1937 and early 1938 in Europe, mainly in Vienna, learning the importing business. After Germany invaded Austria in March 1938, he returned to the United States and enrolled at Ursinus College in Pennsylvania, where he spent one desultory semester in 1938–1939, writing vignettes and brief movie reviews for campus publications. He did not break into a professional writing career until spring 1939, when he enrolled in an evening class in short-story writing taught by Whit Burnett, the editor of the influential *Story* magazine, at Columbia University.

Burnett, who was responsible for the first commercial publication of stories by many important midcentury American writers, was also the first to sense Salinger's potential, accepting "The Young Folks" for the March–April 1940 issue of *Story*. Before the end of the next year, Salinger had also placed short short stories with two popular slick magazines, *Collier's* and *Esquire*, as well as an academic quarterly, the *University of Kansas City Review*. During the same period *The New Yorker* accepted "Slight Rebellion Off Madison", about a young man named Holden Morrisey Caulfield, but delayed publication of the downbeat story for five years. Salinger was drafted into the army in 1942, landed on Utah Beach on D day, and participated in five European campaigns before being discharged in 1945.

Salinger Wrote Earlier Versions of the Holden Caulfield Story

The Catcher in the Rye was the culminating project of the first three decades of Salinger's life. After the publication of the novel in 1951, while he still granted brief interviews, Salinger told a reporter that there was a good deal of himself in Holden Caulfield. Yet the novel is not a thinly fictionalized account of the author's experiences. From the environment in which he grew up, Salinger had absorbed the background for his account of a neurotic, idealistic, upper-middle-class New York teenager living in fashionable apartments, attending unrewarding private schools and summer camps, fighting off "phonies," and trying to keep alive a flickering vision of a "nice" place beyond the threatening streets. Salinger obviously endowed his creation with some of his own prejudices and aspirations, but Holden's family—including a younger sister, Phoebe, an older brother, D.B., and a deceased brother, Allie— was quite different from Salinger's own. He has rarely mentioned his only sibling, an older sister, and she refuses to talk about him. His father was a successful but obscure businessman, not a café society lawyer and unsuccessful angel of Broadway shows, like Holden's father.

An early version of Holden Caulfield, William Jameson Junior in "The Young Folks" is more socially inept, less sensitive, less bedeviled, and less sympathetically presented than Holden. Yet William's language is Holden's. Salinger had already found the distinctive voice that is one of the most compelling reasons for the reputation of *The Catcher in the Rye*. It would take him a while to fashion the character.

Salinger may have named him as early as 1941, when he sold "Slight Rebellion Off Madison" to *The New Yorker*. . . .

Before "Slight Rebellion Off Madison" was finally published, another, somewhat older Holden Caulfield had lived in Salinger's published fiction and may have died in World War II. In "Last Day of the Last Furlough"—a story praised by Ernest Hemingway when the admiring Salinger met him in Paris in August 1944—Vincent Caulfield mentions his younger brother Holden as a twenty-year-old missing in action. Vincent says he used to bump into him at a New York "beer joint for college kids and prep-school kids," where he was "the noisiest, tightest kid in the place." Readers learn little more about him in this story or in "This Sandwich Has No Mayonnaise", probably written during the war and published in the October 1945 issue of *Esquire*. Here it is reported that he was only nineteen when "he came through the war in Europe without a scratch," but he was then shipped out to the Pacific, where he is missing in action. The most important link to *The Catcher in the Rye* is the distraught Vincent's characterization of his brother as a "dope" who "can't reduce a thing to a humor, kill it off with a sarcasm, can't do anything but listen hectically to the maladjusted little apparatus he wears for a heart." Holden is not mentioned in "The Stranger", which conveys the news of Vincent's death on the battlefield. The only sibling mentioned in the story is a younger brother Kenneth, who died as a child (a probable forerunner of Allie in *The Catcher in the Rye*).

In "I'm Crazy", . . . Holden appears as a troubled adolescent. This Holden attends a school called Pentey Prep. (Holden's school in the novel is Pencey Prep.) Each also has a younger sister, Phoebe, in whom he confides, while the Holden of "I'm Crazy" also has an even younger sister, Viola, who is not mentioned elsewhere in Salinger's fiction. . . .

"I'm Crazy" is the earliest published piece of Salinger's fiction that Holden narrates in the first-person voice used in the novel. The first two episodes of this three-thousand-word story were greatly expanded for use in chapters 1 and 2 of *The Catcher in the Rye*. The third and final episode of the story was entirely rewritten as chapters 21 and 22. Despite the close relationship of episodes in this story and the novel, the Holden of "I'm Crazy" is not the same character who appears in the novel. He is simply drifting from day to day, whereas the Holden in the novel has a vision, however impractical and fanciful. "I'm Crazy" is a strictly traditional story of reconciliation with one's unprepossessing destiny, and its protagonist is not a rebel. He is a nice, polite, confused boy who cannot meet the demands of his fashionable, upwardly mobile parents. His problem is not that he will not conform to a self-seeking, materialistic society, but that he cannot. The Holden Caulfield of *The Catcher in the Rye* is someone else. During the interval between World War II and the Korean War, Salinger reshaped his narrative and transformed Holden from one of the multitude, who accept defeat and become another statistic in the lonely crowd, to an individual who struggles to maintain his integrity even if victory is uncertain.

The Publication of *The Catcher in the Rye*

Although Salinger could have published his novelette in 1945, he decided to revise it, and Holden Caulfield was not seen in Salinger's fiction again until the appearance of *The Catcher in the Rye* five and a half years later. During this period there were many changes in Salinger's life and work that influenced him in reworking and expanding the Holden Caulfield story. Salinger had continued to pursue publication in *The New Yorker* even while he was serving in the military. In October 1944 Louise Bogan, poetry adviser to the magazine, wrote to William Maxwell [a *New Yorker* staff member] that a Sergeant Salinger "has been bombarding me with poems for a week or so," by airmail from France. Apparently she was unimpressed, since she asked Salinger's agent for help in stemming the tide. At that time Salinger was in the Hürtgen Forest near Luxembourg preparing to take part in fierce combat as the Germans made a last-ditch stand to turn back the Allies. After that battle Salinger was hospitalized for some time for a nervous condition. It was apparently then that he met his first wife, Sylvia, a French doctor whom he married in September 1945. Little information exists about this marriage, which had ended by July 1946, when Salinger wrote to a friend that his wife had decided to return to France and divorce him. The letter was sent from the Daytona Plaza Hotel in Daytona Beach, Florida, a hostelry that resembles the setting of "A Perfect Day for Bananafish", which seems to draw on Salinger's experiences and feelings at that time. That story, published in the 31 January 1948 issue of *The New Yorker*, was the first of three stories the magazine accepted in 1948. By the time *The Catcher in the Rye* appeared in 1951, Salinger had become known as a "*New Yorker* writer."

William Faulkner once paid Salinger the compliment of calling him the best of "the present generation of writing" because *The Catcher in the Rye* "expresses so completely" what Faulkner himself had tried to say about the tragedy of a youth who found "when he attempted to enter the human race, . . . there was no human race there." Later, however, Faulkner expressed the reservation that there was only enough material in the book for a short story. Faulkner is right in the sense that the first 220 pages provide a background for the fast-moving action of the last 50. The long, episodic buildup in *The Catcher in the Rye* is essential, however, to create a rapport between Holden and the reader.

Holden Returns to His Family's Apartment

Leaving school early, Holden has a series of adventures and misadventures in New York that are akin to the archetypal night journey as rite of passage into maturity. This portion of the novel culminates with Holden's return to his family's apartment, where he finds Phoebe home alone. Holden's problem with growing up is that taking on adult responsibility is fraught with uncertainties. When Phoebe asks him if he would like to be a lawyer like their father, he expresses the fear of the "phoniness" that has haunted him throughout the novel. He says lawyers are "all right if they go around saving innocent guys' lives all the time, . . . but you don't *do* that kind of stuff if you're a lawyer. . . . And besides. Even if you *did* go around saving guys' lives and all, how would you know if you did it because you really *wanted* to save guys' lives, or . . . what you *really* wanted to do was be a terrific lawyer, with everybody

Author J.D. Salinger was best known for his novel The Catcher in the Rye. The Library of Congress.

slapping you on the back and congratulating you. . . ?" "How would you know you weren't being a phony?" he asks and answers: "The trouble is, you *wouldn't*." The only prospect that pleases him is the unrealistic one of keeping children from growing up and—in the process of this guardianship—remaining childlike himself. Holden confesses to Phoebe that he wants only to be a "catcher in the rye" protecting little children from falling off "some crazy cliff." Some readers have interpreted this confession as the climactic revelation of the novel, expressing the vision that Holden will cling to for the rest of his life. Yet he changes his mind completely the next day, when his own childhood ends in a loss of innocence, the sort of "fall" he had hoped to prevent as "catcher in the rye."

Even before Holden finishes explaining himself to Phoebe, she jolts his immature self-confidence by informing him schoolmarmishly that he has not gotten the line from Robert Burns's poem right; in it a body *meets* a body "coming through the rye," allowing the other individual to pass by. Holden will not abandon his private version of the line immediately, for it seems the perfect metaphor to express his thoughts.

Holden Seeks Refuge with Mr. Antolini

After he flees the family apartment to avoid confronting his parents, Holden's faith in his ability to spot phonies is put to the test. He seeks refuge and a night's rest at the apartment of Mr. Antolini, whom Holden considers the best and bravest teacher he has ever had. Antolini fears that Holden is headed for a terrible fall and asks him to ponder a statement by Austrian psychoanalyst Wilhelm Stekel (1868–1940): "The mark of the immature man is that he wants to die nobly for a cause while the mark of the mature man is that he wants to live humbly for one." This piece of advice appears irrelevant in Holden's situation, because Holden has shown no inclination to put his life on the line for anything. Antolini is further discredited as a source of help when, later that night, Holden is suddenly wakened by Antolini, who is patting him on the head. Taking this gesture as a sign of homosexual intention,

Holden runs out of the apartment. After a hard night on a bench in Grand Central Station (which he advises readers to avoid as depressing), Holden wonders whether he could have been wrong about Antolini, "if maybe he just liked to pat guys on the head when they're asleep. I mean how can you tell about that stuff for sure? You can't." Critics' speculations about Antolini's intentions have tended to distract attention from the importance of this episode to the development of Holden's point of view. Salinger may well be suggesting that the mark of maturity is neither living humbly nor dying nobly for a cause but rather struggling to develop an open mind instead of fixedly maintaining a closed one.

Shortly after his second thoughts about Antolini, Holden becomes frightened by the idea of disappearing while crossing a street, a fear that goes back to the opening pages of the novel and to "I'm Crazy". The fear becomes a phobia as Holden starts to call desperately for his dead brother, Allie, to save him. This terror is related to Holden's frenzied behavior when Allie died, as well as to another recurrent motif that also appeared first in "I'm Crazy"—Holden's concern about what happens to the ducks when the lake freezes over in Central Park. Having decided never to return to home or school again, Holden is afraid he may disappear with the ducks. He pleads with Allie not because he wants to join him in death, but because he wants Allie to help him make his way in this world.

Holden Experiences His "Fortunate Fall"

Holden's concern for the world leads to an episode in which the words "fuck you" appear six times. This episode has resulted in some of the most serious misunderstandings of the novel and has led some to attempts to ban the book and prevent schoolchildren from reading it. Yet Holden never uses these words himself. Indeed each time he sees the words scrawled in a public place he is driven into the same kind of frenzy that he felt after Allie's death, and he tries to remove the obscenity before a young child like Phoebe can see it. At first he succeeds, but when he encounters the words scratched in stone, he realizes his crusade is hopeless.

Shortly after the crushing defeat of his attempt to purify the world to which small children are exposed, Holden experiences the fall that Antolini anticipated. Holden goes into a men's room, having decided in disgust that there is no "nice" place. He passes out and collapses on the floor. Believing he could have killed himself in the fall, he recovers and feels better. He has survived. He has experienced "a fortunate fall" into the understanding that he is responsible only to himself.

This awareness is immediately challenged, however, when he meets Phoebe and is troubled to learn that she wants to run away with him. He can change her mind only by going home with her after she rides the Central Park carousel. The idea of experiencing a fall is stressed as Holden watches the children grabbing for the gold (actually brass) ring, just beyond easy reach. Although he fears that Phoebe may fall off her horse, he says nothing. He has forsaken his vision of being catcher in the rye because he now recognizes that "The thing with kids is, if they want to grab for the gold ring, you have to let them do it, and not say anything. If they fall off, they fall off, but it's bad if you say anything to them." He knows now that people cannot be sheltered from all temptations; they must take responsibility for themselves.

This precept may be more easily perceived than applied, for as the brief last chapter of the novel implies, Holden is still torn between minding his own business and meddling in others' lives. When one psychoanalyst asks him whether he will apply himself when he goes back to school, he cannot tell. He has learned how to live with other people, and in so doing he has begun "missing everybody"; but he has no idea yet of what he is going to do with himself. He has an open mind. Salinger has left Holden in an ambiguous state of maturity, with his future openended.

The Catcher in the Rye Becomes a Classic

When *The Catcher in the Rye* was published in July 1951, reviews were generally good. . . . Yet no reviewer foresaw its becoming the classic novel of a generation. It would be five years before academics began writing about the novel and assigning it to their students. By 1968, however, it was listed as one of the top twenty-five American best-sellers since 1895. In the late 1980s it was still selling about a quarter of a million copies per year.

Several times before he completed *The Catcher in the Rye* Salinger himself expressed doubts about ever writing a novel, calling himself essentially a short-story writer; and he has never published a second novel. Yet many critics have treated his stories about the Glass family—including the four long stories collected in *Franny and Zooey* (1961) and *Raise High the Roof Beam, Carpenters and Seymour: An Introduction* (1963)—as parts of a novel. His first published story about a member of the Glass family was the 1948 *New Yorker* story "A Perfect Day for Bananafish". Although he was still working on the final version of Holden Caulfield's story, Salinger's concerns had already begun to turn from the problems of young outsiders growing up in a phony world to the evocation of an idealized "poet-seer." . . .

Salinger Embraces Zen Buddhism

In letters written to friends before he set off on a trip to Florida and Mexico in March 1952, Salinger hinted that something momentous had happened to him, and on his return he urged his British publisher to bring out a complete text of the thousand-page gospels of Hindu mystic Sri Ramakrishna, a propagator of the Advaita Vedanta system of thought, first propounded by Shankaracharya around the eighth century. Salinger subsequently became associated with the Ramakrishna-Vivekananda Center in New York. Salinger's new interest is alluded to in "De Daumier-Smith's Blue Period", published in the May 1952 issue of the British magazine *World Review*. The title character is a painter about Salinger's age who has an extraordinary experience that strikes him as "having been quite transcendent" and leads to a reversal of his previous lifestyle. No particular system of Eastern thought is emphasized in the story. De Daumier-Smith's experience has been compared to a Zen Buddhist satori (moment of temporary illumination), but [critic] Eberhard Alsen argues persuasively that the artist's epiphany ought rather to be compared to the experience of Saint Paul on the road to Damascus in the Acts of the Apostles, where a blinding flash of light leads to his conversion.

Salinger does mention Vedanta in "Teddy". When a young educator asks the ten-year-old title character whether he believes the Vedantic theory of reincarnation, he is politely informed that it is not a theory. Teddy then goes on to explain that in his immediately preceding life he was making a nice spiritual advancement until he met a lady who disrupted his meditations. Salinger commented unfavorably about "Teddy" in "Seymour: An Introduction," where he attributes the tale to his alter ego Buddy Glass and calls it "an exceptionally haunting, memorable, unpleasantly controversial, and thoroughly unsuccessful short story about a 'gifted little boy' aboard a transatlantic liner." When Teddy tries to explain how close he is to final illumination, he admits that in his previous incarnation, even if he had not met the disruptive lady, he was not spiritually advanced enough to go straight to Brahma. "But," he continues, "I wouldn't have had to get incarnated in an *American* body if I hadn't met that lady. I mean it's very hard to meditate and live a spiritual life in America. People think you're a freak if you try to." He also accurately foresees his own death: pushed into an empty swimming pool by his little sister, he dies of a fractured skull. Teddy's dilemma is the same as Seymour's in "A Perfect Day for Bananafish". In a sense Salinger has come back to where he started, failing to break out of the circle. It was time for a fresh start.

Salinger Moves to Cornish, N.H.

On New Year's Day 1953, his thirty-fourth birthday, Salinger moved to the kind of "nice place" that a discouraged Holden Caulfield sought and despaired of finding, the hills of Cornish, New Hampshire, in the upper valley of the Connecticut River. He has lived there ever since. For exactly two years following the appearance of "Teddy", he published no new fiction. *Nine Stories* (1953), which includes the four stories just discussed as well as the widely anthologized "For Esmé—With Love and Squalor", was published in April 1953, with a Zen koan for an epigraph: "We know the sound of two hands clapping / But what is the sound of one hand clapping?" *Nine Stories* went through nine printings before the end of the year, an extraordinary record for a collection of short stories in the United States after World War II.

During his first years in Cornish, Salinger gathered about him a group of high-school students; but their parties began to break up when one of them wrote a short article about him for the *Claremont Daily Eagle*. One day some of the teenagers arrived at his house and found it surrounded by a tall wooden fence. Soon after his arrival in Cornish Salinger had met Claire Douglas, a nineteen-year-old student at Radcliffe College of Harvard University and the daughter of a British art critic who had moved with his family to New York after the outbreak of World War II. Their courtship was interrupted by her brief marriage to a Harvard business major; but on 17 February 1955 she and Salinger were married, and he began to lead an even more secluded life than before.

Just three weeks before the wedding, "Franny", Salinger's first new story in two years, appeared in *The New Yorker* and received the kind of reception usually reserved for major news events. It was also seriously misunderstood, widening the already yawning gap between Salinger and academic critics. . . .

A Shift in Style

"Raise High the Roof Beam, Carpenters" and the few published stories that followed it differ from Salinger's earlier writings in the leisurely manner in which they unfold. Some critics find this meandering technique self-indulgent, but it offers the advantage of clarifying the significance of every detail. The reader is not required to absorb a rapid barrage of subtle details as in many *New Yorker* stories; and it is noteworthy that this story was [chosen] over others—including the much admired "For Esmé—with Love and Squalor"—for inclusion in *Stories from the New Yorker, 1950–1960* (1960), the last anthology of this kind in which Salinger would permit his work to appear.

This mellow, relaxed style was likely a result of the practice of Vedantic meditation, which Seymour recommends in his journals. The development of this new style may also be related to the Salingers' secluded lifestyle in New Hampshire. Their daughter, Margaret Ann, and son, Matthew, were born in 1955 and 1960 respectively, while Salinger was engrossed in the creation of the Glass family legend. What "Raise High the Roof Beam, Carpenters" leads up to is not the surprise announcement that Seymour and Muriel have eloped because Seymour cannot stand all the fashionable rituals of a society wedding, but rather Seymour's concept of marriage, which Buddy reads in Seymour's journal after the news of his elopement and which Salinger wrote while expecting the birth of his first child. Seymour had written, "I've been reading a miscellany of Vedanta all day. Marriage partners are to serve each other. Elevate, help, teach, strengthen each other, but above all, *serve*. Raise their children honorably, lovingly, and with detachment. A child is a guest in the house, to be loved and respected—never possessed, since he belongs to God.". . .

In 1967 Salinger and Claire Salinger divorced. The children continued to visit Cornish at times. Word occasionally leaked out that Salinger was still writing steadily but had no plans for publication. When two pirated volumes of his uncollected stories appeared in 1974, Salinger denounced the publication as "a terrible invasion of my privacy." . . .

In November 1986 Salinger blocked the publication of an unauthorized biography by Ian Hamilton, on the grounds that Hamilton had violated Salinger's copyright by quoting without permission from Salinger letters that their recipients had donated to various libraries. Hamilton then paraphrased the passages he had quoted, but Salinger took him to court anyway, claiming that he had copyrighted the information in the letters as well as the exact words. A federal judge ruled in Hamilton's favor but blocked distribution of the book pending appeal. On 29 January 1987 a U.S. Court of Appeals judge reversed the lower court's decision, stating that Hamilton's paraphrases violated copyright law. In 1988 Hamilton published *In Search of J.D. Salinger*, in which he neither quotes nor paraphrases any of the letters.

After all the publicity surrounding his suit against Hamilton, Salinger continued to guard his privacy. When a serious fire occurred at his Cornish home on 20 October 1992, uninvited visitors were rigorously barred from the property. The most surprising information in *The New York Times* account of the fire was the identification of his spokesperson as his "considerably younger" third wife, Colleen O'Neill. No further information about her or their marriage has been forthcoming.

Salinger may have explained his obsessive desire for privacy in *The Catcher in the Rye* where Holden describes a short story by his older brother D.B. In "The Secret Goldfish," Holden says, "this little kid . . . wouldn't let anybody look at his goldfish because he'd bought it with his own money." The novel in which this passage appeared put Salinger in a position to pay for his own privacy in Cornish, New Hampshire.

J.D. Salinger as a *New Yorker* Writer

David L. Stevenson

David L. Stevenson was a writer who contributed to The Na-tion.

In the following essay, David L. Stevenson discusses how J.D. Salinger is identified as a New Yorker writer, a style of writing that has city wit infused with prose and stylized irony. Salinger's stories revolve around a plot concentrating on two to three char-acters, and focuses on a certain crisis in the character's lives. The main focus on Salinger's stories is indeed the crisis, which is written in such a way that makes a reader aware of his or her own problems, relating to the characters.

[In an overview of Salinger's fiction, Stevenson suggests that Salinger's short stories are powerful because they ac-curately reflect the emotional predicament of men and women in modern society.]

New Yorker Writer

Because of [his] diffidence to things dedicatedly literary, Salin-ger is usually identified by book reviewers, and properly, as a *New Yorker* writer, implying thereby both city wit and surface brilliance in his use of prose and stylized irony of situation in his use of plot. . . .

Salinger is surely one of the most skillful practitioners of the *New Yorker* short story or sketch. And, invidious critics aside, his sketches show it to be, at its best, one of the truly distinctive and definable fictional types of mid-century Ameri-can letters. This kind of story contains no more than two or

David L. Stevenson, "J.D. Salinger: The Mirror of Crisis," The *Nation*, March 9, 1957. Reproduced by permission.

three characters, seen always at a moment of crisis in one of their lives. The concentration is on the crisis: the relationships which have led to it are indistinct, only suggested by the tone of the dialogue, by characters' momentary actions and gestures. The Salinger-*New Yorker* story is always a kind of closet scene between Hamlet and his mother with the rest of the play left out. It accomplishes its shock of surprise, and it evokes our emotions, by a frugal underplaying of plot and event, by its very minimizing of narrative. The reader is usually not projected into the problems of its characters because he is not given enough of the fabric of their lives to make such projection possible.

What a Salinger story *does* involve the reader in is something quite different. It is his awareness that the crisis of the sketch is a generic one of our time and place. The crisis of the usual *New Yorker* story may be fairly casual, and we have come to expect a Salinger story to be more stern in its implications because its roots are stronger and probe more deeply. But its crisis runs true to form. Salinger does not take you out of yourself into a living, substantial world of fiction. He throws you back into your own problems, or into an awareness of them in your contemporaries. His characters do not exist in a rich narrative, in a detailed setting, so that they become wholly separable, fictional beings. Rather they give us a feeling of our own sensitivity to compensate for their lack of created density.

Characters Shape the Stories

One can best illustrate this quality of a Salinger story by comparing his *New Yorker* sketch "Pretty Mouth and Green My Eyes" [from *Nine Stories*] with Hemingway's "The Short Happy Life of Francis Macomber." The two stories offer the same basic character relationships: passively suffering husband, aggressively lustful wife, and casual, opportunistic lover. In Hemingway's version, however, the characters are embedded in a full, complex plot in which motive and event are made inexorably overt. The tensions of the characters are in open balance for the reader, and the husband's declared failure of nerve is what provokes his wife's ruthless retaliation in taking a lover. The Macombers exist in the round as "created" individuals in a self-contained narrative which could be translated into mandarin and remain comprehensible.

Part of the virtue of "Pretty Mouth and Green My Eyes," on the other hand, is that it is not a self-contained narrative. We know of the characters only that they are apartment dwellers in New York. They exist as voices on a telephone to illustrate the desperate irony of a husband calling his wife's latest lover, after a party the three of them have attended, at the moment when the lover is in bed with the wife. The tearing crisis of the story is the husband's slow realization, as he complains in hideously maudlin, drunken terms of his wife's infidelities, that he has put his own self-respect beyond the point of salvage. Salinger's characters, here, come alive *New Yorker* fashion through the skillful verisimilitude of their conversation . . . . They are important to us in direct proportion to our recognition of them as generic sketches of our urban, childless, apartmented men and women, alienated by the hectic nature of their lives from all quiet interflow of love and affection.

One significant element in the structure of a Salinger story, then, and a source of his power over us, is that his characters come alive in our recognition of them. In complementary fashion, an equally significant element is the effect on us of the special kind of crisis he asks us to identify. As in "Pretty Mouth and Green My Eyes," it is a crisis in a character's life that results from an erosion of personality peculiar to upper middle-class, mid-century America. It is related to our sense of the heightened vulnerability of men and women to emotional disaster.

Emotional Estrangement

I am not prepared to argue that the Salinger species of crisis is unique, and that other ages did not feel themselves alienated from inner security and outward affection. *Hamlet* alone would suffice. I should only assert that in our time and place, the individual estranged from his fellows seems peculiarly understandable and therefore touching to us. . . .

Salinger's short stories are all variations on the theme of emotional estrangement. In "Down at the Dinghy," a small boy runs away when he overhears his father referred to as a "kike." In "Uncle Wiggily in Connecticut," two women, unsuccessful adventurers in love, let a Connecticut afternoon drift away on highballs and reminiscences, while the timid child of one of them retreats farther and farther into compensatory fantasy as the two women get progressively more sodden. In "A Perfect Day for Bananafish" a young soldier released from an army hospital confronts his wife's complicated indifference during their first reunion. When he is forced to weigh a small child's warm, intuitive sympathy against his wife's society prettiness, he shoots himself. The actions of the characters in all these stories could seem arbitrary, judged by the sketchiness of Salinger's narrative. In fact, however, the actions seem real and shocking because they are the kind of thing we can anticipate from the needs and stresses we share at least in part with the characters. . . .

Shaping Style and Tone with Imagination

There is a further fictional device used . . . in [Salinger's] short stories. . . . It is his use of almost Chaplin-like incidents and dialogue, half-amusing, half-desperate, to keep his story always hovering in ambivalence between comedy and tragedy. Whenever a character approaches hopelessness in a Salinger sketch, he is getting there by the route of the comic. It is usually both the character's way of holding on for a moment longer (as when the husband in "A Perfect Day for Bananafish" goes out of his way to insult a proper dowager just before he kills himself) and, at its sharpest, a way of dramatic irony, a way of heightening the intensity of a character's predicament (as when Holden [in *The Catcher in the Rye*] attempts to be bored with sex to get rid of a prostitute). . . .

When one is reading Salinger, one accepts his carefully placed "New Yorkerish" style and tone, and surrenders one's mind almost completely. It is only when you put the story aside and turn to other contemporary writers and to other fictional methods and techniques that you begin to wonder whether the immediacy and vividness of Salinger might be limited in power. Nowhere in Salinger do we find ourselves plunged into the emotional coiling and recoiling provoked by passages from Styron's novel, *Lie Down in Darkness*. Nowhere in Salinger is a character moved against the murky intensity-in-depth of a Nelson Algren Chicago scene, in *The Man with the Golden Arm*. Nowhere is a character revealed by the great clots of heterogeneous detail yoked together in single crowded sentences, as by Saul Bellow in *The Adventures of Augie March*.

But despite the temptations of comparison there remains one's conviction that Salinger is deeply and seriously committed in his fiction. Further, a little research into the Salinger canon reveals that two of his major creations, Holden Caulfield and Seymour Glass, the young husband of "A Perfect Day for Bananafish," have deep roots in Salinger's own imagination. His novel, in its way, is as much a final version of "work in progress" as are the novels of his more literary contemporaries, pulled together from fragmentary excursions as short stories in *Partisan Review*, in *Hudson Review*, in *New World Writing*. Only with Salinger, the professional, early sketches of Holden Caulfield occur in a series of stories published in *The Saturday Evening Post*, *Collier's*, and in the *New Yorker*, in the years 1944–1946. And Seymour Glass turns out to have rich interconnections in Salinger's mind with the uncle of the runaway boy of "Down at the Dinghy," with the older brother of the heroine in a sketch "Franny," and with the bridegroom in a novelette "Raise High the Roof Beam, Carpenters."

This extrinsic information helps verify one's feeling that there is actually more weight to his explorations of human alienation than his bright dialogue and his frugal use of background and event might suggest. Moreover, Salinger's nonliterary status leaves him, as a serious writer, almost unique as a wholly free agent, unhampered by the commitments of his more dedicated contemporaries to one or another school of critics. One might guess that this is Salinger's most precious asset. Rather than wishing quarterly significance or "greatness" on him, we can be content to take him for what he is: a beautifully deft, professional performer who gives us a chance to catch quick, half-amused, half-frightened glimpses of ourselves and our contemporaries, as he confronts us with his brilliant mirror images. . . .

The Catcher in the Rye and Depression

Holden Caulfield Is Disgusted by Phoniness

Harrison Smith

Harrison Smith, an editor and publisher, was president of the Saturday Review of Literature.

In this early review of The Catcher in the Rye, *Harrison Smith finds it a remarkable novel and superior to the work of many young writers writing about the youth of the day with despair and bitterness. He sees Holden Caulfield's battle against the phoniness that surrounds him as pathetic, rather than tragic, and praises Salinger for the unique, original voice he has created for Holden. Smith asserts that, although the novel depicts an unusually sensitive young man, it also provides insight into the way that all children encounter the complexities of the modern world.*

That there is something wrong or lacking in the novels of despair and frustration that many of our younger writers are turning out has long been apparent. The sour note of bitterness and the recurring theme of sadism have become almost a convention, never thoroughly explained by the author's dependence on a psychoanalytical interpretation of a major character. The boys who are spoiled or turned into budding homosexuals by their mothers and a loveless home life are as familiar to us today as stalwart and dependable young heroes were to an earlier generation. We have accepted this interpretation of the restlessness and bewilderment of our young men and boys because no one had anything better to offer. It is tragic to hear the anguished cry of parents: "What have we done to harm him? Why doesn't he care about anything? He is a bright boy, but why does he fail to pass his examinations? Why won't he talk to us?"

Harrison Smith, "Manhattan Ulysses, Junior," *The Saturday Review of Literature*, vol. XXXIV, July 14, 1951, pp. 12–13.

Holden Caulfield Is Pathetic, but Not Hopeless

A remarkable and absorbing novel has appeared, J.D. Salinger's "The Catcher in the Rye," which may serve to calm the apprehensions of fathers and mothers about their own responsibilities, though it does not attempt to explain why all boys who dismay their elders have failed to pass successfully the barrier between childhood and young manhood. It is a profoundly moving and a disturbing book, but it is pathetic rather than tragic, and it is not hopeless. Holden Caulfield, sixteen years old and six foot two inches in height, narrates his own story from the time when he was dismissed from his third private school to return, ill and in a state of physical and mental shock, to the shelter of his home in New York three days later. What happens to him is heart-rending. To many readers some of his words and the accidents that befall him may seem to be too raw to be expressed in the words of a childish youth. If readers can be shocked in this manner they should be advised to let the book alone.

What was wrong with Holden was his moral revulsion against anything that was ugly, evil, cruel, or what he called "phoney" and his acute responsiveness to beauty and innocence, especially the innocence of the very young, in whom he saw reflected his own lost childhood. The book is full of the voices and the delightful antics of children. Especially he adored his stalwart and understanding little sister, who in the end undoubtedly saved him from suicide. And there were the memories of his dead brother, whom he had loved, and a teacher in the first school from which he was dismissed. He had no other friends, dead or alive. He accepted his parents, whose union had been happy, as one of the stable factors in a devastating world. When he ran away from school he knew that he had three days before they would hear of his dismissal from the headmaster. His desire to escape from the ordeal of their disappointment in him and to hide in New York, to go underground, is understandable. Not every boy would have done it, but the reader is convinced that Holden would and that his behavior throughout the book is equally natural and inevitable.

The Authenticity of the Language Is Powerful

The magic of this novel does not depend on this boy's horrifying experience but on the authenticity of the language he uses and the emotions and memories which overwhelm him. Without realizing it he is seeking the understanding and affection which adults could give him—or even his classmates, who are perhaps an unreasonably repulsive lot of lads. But how could they be fond of this overgrown, precocious, and yet childish boy? His roommate was an arrogant hunter of girls; the boy next door never brushed his teeth and was always picking at his pimples; the group of "intellectuals," the grinds, and the athletes were all phonies to him. But Holden's sense of the phoniness is never contempt. It is worse; it is despair. . . .

"The Catcher in the Rye" is not all horror. . . . There is a wry humor in this sixteen-year-old's trying to live up to his height, to drink with men, to understand mature sex and why he is still a virgin at his age. His affection for children is spontaneous and delightful. There are few little girls in modern fiction as charming and lovable as his little sister, Phoebe. Altogether this is a book to be read thoughtfully and more than once. It is about an unusually sensitive and intelligent boy; but, then, are not all boys unusual and worthy of understanding? If they are bewildered at the complexity of modern life, unsure of themselves, shocked by the spectacle of perversity and evil around them—are not adults equally shocked by the knowledge that even children cannot escape this contact and awareness?

Holden Caulfield Is Searching for Love

Arthur Heiserman and James E. Miller Jr.

James E. Miller Jr. is the author of numerous literary biographies and works of literary criticism, including J.D. Salinger. He was at one time the editor of College English *and is the Helen A. Regenstein Professor Emeritus of English at the University of Chicago. Arthur Heiserman was a professor of English at the University of Chicago.*

In this seminal early essay on The Catcher in the Rye, *Arthur Heiserman and James E. Miller Jr. identify the novel as belonging to the tradition of the quest, in which the hero embarks on an epic journey. Unlike most American heroes of fiction, who are wanderers seeking to leave their homes for new frontiers, Holden Caulfield is seeking both to leave home and to return to the security of his home. The authors contend that the central theme of all of Salinger's work is the hell of being unable to love. Holden Caulfield has the capacity to love, but the only world he finds worthy of his love is the world of childhood innocence. To be cured of his depression, the authors assert, he must be pushed over the "crazy cliff" into a phony adult world.*

It is clear that J.D. Salinger's *The Catcher in the Rye* belongs to an ancient and honorable narrative tradition, perhaps the most profound in western fiction. The tradition is the central pattern of the epic and has been enriched by every tongue; for not only is it in itself exciting but also it provides the artist a framework upon which he may hang almost any fabric of events and characters.

It is, of course, the tradition of the Quest. . . .

Arthur Heiserman and James E. Miller Jr., "J.D. Salinger: Some Crazy Cliff," *Western Humanities Review*, vol. X, Spring 1956, pp. 129–137.

The Tradition of the Quest

There are at least two sorts of quests . . . the one seeking acceptance and stability, the other precisely the opposite . . . a Truth which is unwarped by stability.

American literature seems fascinated with the outcast, the person who defies traditions in order to arrive at some pristine knowledge, some personal integrity. Natty Bumppo [protagonist in James Fenimore Cooper's *Leatherstocking Tales*] maintains his integrity out-of-doors only, for upon the frontier a man must be a man or perish. For Huck Finn [title character in Mark Twain's *Adventures of Huckleberry Finn*] both sides of the Mississippi are lined with fraud and hatred; and because the great brown river acts as a kind of sewer, you're liable to find murderers and thieves afloat on it—even the father whom you fled might turn up dead in it, as though the river were a dream. But in the middle of the great natural river, when you're naked of civilization and in company with an outcast more untarnished and childlike than yourself—*there* is peace. And in northern Mississippi, in the ante-Snopes [a family of unpleasant people in various novels by William Faulkner] era, frontiersmen conquer the wilderness using only their courage and their fury; and they behave, even when civilization has almost extinguished them, with the kind of insane honor that drives Quentin Compson [a character in Faulkner's novels *The Sound and the Fury* and *Absalom, Absalom!*] outside of society and into suicide. . . .

All the virtues of these American heroes are personal ones: they most often, as a matter of fact, are in conflict with home, family, church. The typical American hero must flee these institutions, become a tramp in the earth, cut himself off from Chicago, Winesburg, Hannibal, Cooperstown, New York, Asheville, Minneapolis. For only by flight can he find knowledge of what is real. And if he does not flee, he at least defies.

The protagonist of *The Catcher in the Rye*, Holden Caulfield, is one of these American heroes, but with a significant difference. He seems to be engaged in both sorts of quests at once; he needs to go home and he needs to leave it. Unlike the other American knight errants, Holden seeks Virtue second to Love. He wants to be good. When the little children are playing in the rye-field on the clifftop, Holden wants to be the one who catches them before they fall off the cliff. He is not driven toward honor or courage. He is not driven toward love of woman. Holden is driven toward love of his fellow-man, charity—virtues which were perhaps not quite verile [sic] enough for Natty Bumppo, Ishmael [the narrator of Herman Melville's *Moby Dick*] Huck Finn, or Nick Adams [a character in Ernest Hemingway's *The Nick Adams Stories*]. Holden is actually frightened by a frontier code of masculinity—a code which sometimes requires its adherents to behave in sentimental and bumptious fashions. But like these American heroes, Holden is a wanderer, for in order to be good he has to be more of a bad boy than the puritanical Huck could have imagined. Holden has had enough of both Hannibal, Missouri, *and* the Mississippi; and his tragedy is that when he starts back up the river, he has no place to go—save, of course, a California psychiatrist's couch.

Holden Caulfield Is Seeking Love

So Salinger translates the old tradition into contemporary terms. The phoniness of society forces Holden Caulfield to leave it, but he is seeking nothing less than stability and love. He would like nothing better than a home, a life embosomed upon what is known and can be trusted; he is a very wise sheep forced into lone wolf's clothing; he is Stephen Dedalus [protagonist of James Joyce's *Portrait of the Artist as a Young Man* and a character in his *Ulysses*] and Leopold Bloom [protagonist of Joyce's *Ulysses*] rolled into one crazy kid. And here is the point; for poor Holden, there is no Ithaca [home of Odysseus in Homer's *Odyssey*]. Ithaca has not merely been defiled by a horde of suitors: it has sunk beneath waves of pho-

Snapshots

"Catcher in the Rye," Cartoon by Jason Love. CartoonStock.com.

niness. He does, of course, have a Penelope [faithful wife of Odysseus] who is still intact. She is his little sister Phoebe whom he must protect at all costs from the phantoms of lust, hypocrisy, conceit and fear—all of the attributes which Holden sees in society and which Huck Finn saw on the banks of the Mississippi and Dedalus saw in Dublin. So at the end . . . Holden delights in circles—a comforting, bounded figure which yet connotes hopelessness. He breaks down as he watches his beloved little Phoebe going round and round on a carousel; she is so *damned* happy. From that lunatic delight in a circle, he is shipped off to the psychiatrist. For Holden loves the world more than the world can bear.

Holden's Quest takes him outside society; yet the grail he seeks is the world and the grail is full of love. To be a catcher in the rye in this world is possible only at the price of leaving it. To be good is to be a "case," a "bad boy" who confounds the society of men. So Holden seeks the one role which would allow him to be a catcher, and that role is the role of the child. As a child, he would be condoned, for a child is a sort of savage and a pariah because he is innocent and good. But it is Holden's tragedy that he is sixteen, and like [William] Wordsworth he can never be less. In childhood he had what he is now seeking—non-phoniness, truth, innocence. He can find it now only in Phoebe and in his dead brother Allie's baseball mitt, in a red hunting cap and the tender little nuns. Still, unlike all of us, Holden refuses to compromise with adulthood and its necessary adulteries; and his heroism drives him berserk. Huck Finn had the Mississippi and at the end of the Mississippi he had the wild west beyond Arkansas. The hero of *The Waste Land* [a poem by T.S. Eliot] had Shantih, the peace which passes human understanding. Bloom had Molly and his own ignorance; Dedalus had Paris and Zurich. But for Holden, there is no place to go.

Salinger's Theme Is the Suffering of Being Unable to Love

The central theme of Salinger's work is stated explicitly in one of his best stories, "For Esmé—with Love and Squalor." Salinger quotes a passage from Dostoevski: "Fathers and teachers, I ponder 'What is Hell?' I maintain that it is the suffering of being unable to love." . . .

This Love must be spelled with a capital; for it is not the alienated, romantic love or the courtly romances and "Dover Beach" [a poem by Matthew Arnold]—a love which is tragic because it is founded upon Eros; but rather it is the expansive, yea-saying love of all Creation which we find in the saints and which is never tragic because it is founded upon Agape [unconditional, usually spiritual, love]. This love is the dominant trait of all Salinger's heroes, and when it is thwarted the hero either shoots himself, as does the veteran with "battle fatigue" in "A Perfect Day for Bananafish," or goes berserk or melancholic as do the heroes of *The Catcher in the Rye* and "Uncle Wiggly in Connecticut." But when, on the other hand, a person finds a way to love the world, then that person is saved from madness and suicide as is the soldier in "For Esmé." Salinger thus diagnoses the neurosis and fatigue of the world in one simple way: if we cannot love, we cannot live. . . .

The Flight into Childhood

The flight out of the world, out of the ordinary, and into an Eden of innocence or childhood is a common flight indeed, and it is one which Salinger's heroes are constantly attempting. But Salinger's childism is consubstantial with his concern for love and neurosis. Adultism is precisely "the suffering of being unable to love," and it is that which produces neurosis. Everyone able to love in Salinger's stories is either a child or a man influenced by a child. All the adults not informed by love and innocence are by definition phonies and prostitutes. "You take adults, they always look lousy when they're asleep with their mouths open, but kids don't. . . . They look all right." Kids like Phoebe shut up when they haven't anything to say. They even say "thank you" when you tighten their skates, and they don't go behind a post to button their pants. The nuns expect no swanky lunches after standing on a corner to collect money. Young James Castle would not go back on his word even though he had to jump from a window to keep it.

Holden is the kind of person who feels sorry for the teachers who have to flunk him. He fears for the ducks when the lagoon freezes over, for he is a duck himself with no place to go. He must enter his own home like a crook, lying to elevator boys and tip-toeing past bedrooms. His dad "will kill" him and his mother will weep for his incorrigible "laziness." He wants only to pretend he is a deaf-mute and live as a hermit filling-station operator in Colorado, but he winds up where the frontier ends, California, in an institution for sick rich kids. And we can see, on the final note of irony in the book, that that frontier west which represented escape from "siviliza-tion" for Huck Finn has ended by becoming the symbol for depravity and phoniness in our national shrine at Hollywood.

The Humor in *Catcher*

The most distinctive aspect of Salinger's humor is its invari-able effect of intensifying poignance and even horror. . . .

It is this poignance which characterizes all of Salinger's humor, this catch in the throat that accompanies all of the laughs. Holden Caulfield is no clown nor is he a tragic hero; he is a sixteen-year-old lad whose vivid encounter with every-day life is tragically humorous—or humorously tragic. At the end of the novel, as we leave Holden in the psychiatric ward of the California hospital, we come to the realization that the abundant and richly varied humor of the novel has reinforced the serious intensity of Holden's frantic flight from Adultism and his frenzied search for the genuine in a terrifyingly phony world.

Holden Caulfield, like Huckleberry Finn, tells his own story and it is in the language of the telling in both books that a great part of the humor lies. In the nineteenth century, Huck began, "You don't know about me without you have read a book by the name of *The Adventures of Tom Sawyer* [novel by Mark Twain]: but that ain't no matter." The English of Huck's twentieth century counterpart, Holden Caulfield, is perhaps more correct but none-the-less distinctive: "If you re-ally want to hear about it, the first thing you'll probably want to know is where I was born, and what my lousy childhood was like, and how my parents were occupied and all before they had me, and all that David Copperfield kind of crap, but I don't feel like going into it, if you want to know the truth."

The skepticism inherent in that casual phrase, "if you want to know the truth," suggesting that as a matter of fact in the world of Holden Caulfield very few people do, characterizes this sixteen-year-old "crazy mixed up kid" more sharply and vividly than pages of character "analysis" possibly could. In a similar manner Huck's "that ain't no matter" speaks volumes for his relationship to the alien adult world in which he finds himself a sojourner. But if these two boys lay their souls bare by their own voices, in doing so they provoke smiles at their mishandling and sometimes downright mangling of the English language.

Huck's spelling of *sivilization* gives the word a look which makes what it stands for understandably distasteful. Holden's incorrectness frequently appears to be a straining after correctness ("She'd give Allie or I a push. . . .") which suggests a subconscious will to non-conformity. But the similarities of language of Huck and Holden are balanced by marked differences. Both boys are fugitives from education, but Holden has suffered more of the evil than Huck. Holden's best subject in the several schools he has tolerated briefly is English. And, too, Holden is a child of the twentieth century. Mark Twain himself would probably be startled not at the frankness of Holden's language but at the daring of J.D. Salinger in copying it so faithfully.

Salinger's Skill as a Narrator

But of course neither J.D. Salinger nor Mark Twain really "copied" anything. Their books would be unreadable had they merely recorded intact the language of a real-life Huck and a real-life Holden. Their genius lies in their mastery of the technique of first person narration which, through meticulous selection, creates vividly the illusion of life: gradually and subtly their narrators emerge and stand revealed, stripped to their innermost beings. It is a mark of their creators' mastery that Huck and Holden appear to reveal themselves.

It is not the least surprising aspect of *The Catcher in the Rye* that trite expressions and metaphors with which we are all familiar and even bored turn out, when emerging from the mouth of a sixteen-year-old, to be funny. The unimaginative repetition of identical expressions in countless situations intensifies the humor. The things in Holden's world are always jumping up and down or bouncing or scattering "like madmen." Holden always lets us know when he has insight into the absurdity of the endless absurd situations which make up the life of a sixteen-year-old by exclaming, [*sic*] "It killed me." In a phony world Holden feels compelled to reenforce his sincerity and truthfulness constantly with, "It really is" or "It really did." Incongruously the adjective "old" serves as a term of endearment, from "old" Thomas Hardy to "old" Phoebe. And many of the things Holden does, he does, ambiguously, "like a bastard."

Holden is a master of the ludicrous irrelevancy. Indeed, a large part of *The Catcher in the Rye* consists of the relevantly irrelevant. On the opening page, Holden says, "I'm not going to tell you my whole goddam autobiography or anything. I'll just tell you about this madman stuff that happened to me around last Christmas. . . ." By the time we have finished *Catcher* we feel that we know Holden as thoroughly as any biography could reveal him, and one of the reasons is that he has not hesitated to follow in his tale wherever whim and fancy lead him. For example, in the early part of the novel, Holden goes at some length into the history of the Ossenburger Memorial Wing of the new dorms, his place of residence. Ossenburger, we are told, was the Pencey alumnus who made a "pot of dough" in the undertaking business, and who, after giving money to Pencey, gave a speech in chapel "that lasted about ten hours." "He told us we should always pray to God—talk to Him and all—wherever we were. He told us we ought to think of Jesus as our buddy and all. He said *he* talked to Jesus all of the time. Even when he was driving his car. That killed me. I can just see the big phony bastard shifting into first gear and asking Jesus to send him a few more stiffs." Ossenburger, of course, has nothing to do, directly, with the "madman stuff" that happened to Holden around Christmas; but Holden's value judgment of the phony Ossenburger is certainly relevant to Salinger's purpose, the revelation of Holden's character.

When Holden refuses to express aggressive dislike of the repulsive Ackley, the pimply boy whose teeth "looked mossy and awful," he is not being facetious nor is he lying. He is simply expressing an innocence incapable of genuine hatred. Holden does not suffer from the inability to love, but he does despair of finding a place to bestow his love. The depth of Holden's capacity for love is revealed in his final words, as he sits in the psychiatric ward musing over his nightmarish adventures: "If you want to know the truth, I don't *know* what I think about it. I'm sorry I told so many people about it. About all I know is, I sort of miss everybody I told about. Even old Stradlater and Ackley, for instance. I think I even miss that goddam Maurice. It's funny. Don't ever tell anybody anything. If you do, you start missing everybody." We agree with Holden that it is funny, but it is funny in a pathetic kind of way. As we leave Holden alone in his room in the psychiatric ward, we are aware of the book's last incongruity. It is not Holden who should be examined for a sickness of the mind, but the world in which he has sojourned and found himself an alien. To "cure" Holden, he must be given the contagious, almost universal disease of phony adultism; he must be pushed over that "crazy cliff."

Holden Caulfield Is Searching for a Father

Jonathan Baumbach

Jonathan Baumbach is a fiction writer, critic, and educator in English and creative writing. His works of criticism include The Landscape of Nightmare: Studies in the Contemporary American Novel.

Jonathan Baumbach maintains that in The Catcher in the Rye, *Holden Caulfield is searching for a spiritual father. He details how the fathers in the novel fail Holden. Baumbach avers that the book is spiritual and that its hero is a child-saint. However, he says, Holden Caulfield is an impotent savior, unable to save the corrupt world that he lives in, and so he retreats into the safe world of childhood.*

Like all of Salinger's fiction, *Catcher in the Rye* is not only about innocence, it is actively for innocence—as if retaining one's childness were an existential possibility. The metaphor of the title—Holden's fantasy-vision of standing in front of a cliff and protecting playing children from falling (Falling)—is, despite the impossibility of its realization, the only positive action affirmed in the novel. It is, in Salinger's Manichean [dualistic] universe of child angels and adult "phonies," the only moral alternative—otherwise all is corruption. Since it is spiritually as well as physically impossible to prevent the Fall, Salinger's idealistic heroes are doomed either to suicide (Seymour [the eldest Glass son, featured in five Salinger works of fiction]), or insanity (Holden, Sergeant X [hero of "For Esmé—with Love and Squalor"]) or mysticism (Franny [the Glass daughter featured in *Franny and Zooey*]), the ways

Jonathan Baumbach, "The Saint as a Young Man: A Reappraisal of The Catcher in the Rye," *Modern Language Quarterly*, vol. 25, December 1964, pp. 461–472.

of sainthood, or to moral dissolution (Eloise [a character in "Uncle Wiggily in Connecticut"], D.B., Mr. Antolini), the way of the world. In Salinger's finely honed prose, at once idiomatically real and poetically stylized, we get the terms of Holden's ideal adult occupation:

> Anyway, I keep picturing all these little kids playing some game in this big field of rye and all. Thousands of little kids, and nobody's around—nobody big, I mean—except me. And I'm standing on the edge of some crazy cliff. What I have to do, I have to catch everybody if they start to go over the cliff—I mean if they're running and they don't look where they're going I have to come out from somewhere and *catch* them. That's all I'd do all day. I'd just be the catcher in the rye and all. I know it's crazy, but that's the only thing I'd really like to be. I know it's crazy.

Holden Caulfield Wants to Be a Saint

Apparently Holden's wish is purely selfless. What he wants, in effect, is to be a saint—the protector and savior of innocence. But what he also wants, for he is still one of the running children himself, is that someone prevent *his* fall. This is his paradox: he must leave innocence to protect innocence. At sixteen, he is ready to shed his innocence and move like Adam into the fallen adult world, but he resists because those no longer innocent seem to him foolish as well as corrupt. In a sense, then, he is looking for an exemplar, a wise-good father whose example will justify his own initiation into manhood. Before Holden can become a catcher in the rye, he must find another catcher in the rye to show him how it is done. . . .

Holden Seeks a Spiritual Father

Holden's real quest throughout the novel is for a spiritual father (an innocent adult). He calls Antolini after all the other fathers of his world have failed him, including his real father, whose existence in the novel is represented solely by Phoebe's childish reiteration of "Daddy's going to kill you." The fathers in Salinger's child's-eye world do not catch falling boys—who have been thrown out of prep school—but "kill" them. Antolini represents Holden's last chance to find a catcher-father. But his inability to save Holden has been prophesied in his failure to save James Castle; the episode of Castle's death provides an anticipatory parallel to Antolini's unwitting destruction of Holden.

That Antolini's kindness to Holden is motivated in part by a homosexual interest, though it comes as a shock to Holden, does not wholly surprise the reader. Many of the biographical details that Salinger has revealed about him through Holden imply this possibility. For example, that he has an older and unattractive wife whom he makes a great show of kissing in public is highly suggestive; yet the discovery itself—Holden wakes to find Antolini sitting beside him and caressing his head—has considerable impact. We experience a kind of shock of recognition, the more intense for its having been anticipated. The scene has added power because Antolini is, for the most part, a good man, whose interest in Holden is genuine as well as perverted. His advice to Holden is apparently well-intentioned. Though many of his recommendations are cleverly articulated platitudes, Antolini evinces a prophetic insight when he tells Holden, "I have a feeling that you're riding for some kind of terrible, terrible fall"; one suspects, however, that to some extent he is talking about himself. Ironically, Antolini becomes the agent of his "terrible, terrible fall" by violating Holden's image of him, by becoming a false father. Having lost his respect for Antolini as a man, Holden rejects him as an authority; as far as Holden is concerned, Antolini's example denies the import of his words. His disillusionment with Antolini, who had seemed to be the sought-for, wise-good father, comes as the most intense of a long line of disenchantments; it is the final straw that breaks Holden. It is the equivalent of the loss of God. The world, devoid of good fathers (authorities), becomes a soul-destroying chaos in which his survival is possible only through withdrawal into childhood, into fantasy, into psychosis. . . .

Holden not only suffers as a victim from the effects of the evil in this world, but for it as its conscience—so that his experiences are exemplary. In this sense, *Catcher in the Rye* is a religious or, to be more exact, spiritual novel. Holden is Prince Mishkin [the central character in Fyodor Dostoevsky's *The Idiot*] as a sophisticated New York adolescent; and like Mishkin, he experiences the guilt, unhappiness, and spiritual deformities of others more intensely than he does his own misfortunes. This is not to say that Holden is without faults; he is, on occasion, silly, irritating, thoughtless, irresponsible—he has the excesses of innocence. Yet he is, as nearly as possible, without sin.

Holden Faces the Loss of Innocence

The most memorable love affair Holden has experienced had its fruition in daily checker games with Jane Gallagher, an unhappy, sensitive girl who was his neighbor one summer. She had become the symbol to him of romantic love, that is, innocent love. When Holden discovers that his "sexy" roommate Stradlater has a date with her, he is concerned not only about the possible loss of Jane's innocence, but about the loss of his dream of her—the loss of their combined checker-playing, love-innocence. Holden has had one previous emotional breakdown at thirteen when his saint-brother, Allie, died of leukemia. In Allie's death, Holden first recognized the fact of evil—of what appears to be the gratuitous malevolence of the universe. Allie, who was, Holden tells us, more intelligent and nicer than anyone else, has become for Holden a kind of saint-ideal. By rejecting an English theme on Allie's baseball glove that Holden has written for him, and by implying that he has "given Jane Gallagher the time," Stradlater spiritually maims Holden. Holden's sole defense, a belief in the possibility of good in the world, collapses: "I felt so lonesome, all of a sudden. I almost wished I was dead."

It is in this state of near-suicidal despair that Holden leaves for New York. That Stradlater may have had sexual relations with Jane—the destruction of innocence is an act of irremediable evil in Holden's world—impels Holden to leave Pencey immediately (but not before he quixotically challenges the muscular Stradlater, who in turn bloodies his nose). At various times in New York, Holden is on the verge of phoning Jane, and actually dials her number twice—that he is unable to reach her is symbolic of his loss of her innocence. The sexually experienced Stradlater, who is one of Holden's destructive fathers in the novel, has destroyed not Jane's innocence so much as Holden's idealized notion of her.

The Adult World Deepens Holden's Despair

Obliquely searching for good in the adult world, or at least something to mitigate his despair, Holden is continually confronted with the absence of good. On his arrival in the city, he is disturbed because his cabdriver is corrupt and unsociable and, worst of all, unable to answer Holden's obsessional question: where do the Central Park ducks go when the lake freezes over? What Holden really wants to know is whether there is a benevolent authority that takes care of ducks. If there is one for ducks, it follows that there may be one for people as well. Holden's quest for a wise and benevolent authority, then, is essentially a search for a God-principle. However, none of the adults in Holden's world has any true answers for him. When he checks into a hotel room, he is depressed by the fact that the bellboy is an old man ("What a gorgeous job for a guy around sixty-five years old"). As sensitized recorder of the moral vibrations of his world, Holden suffers the indignity of the aged bellhop's situation for him, as he had suffered for Spencer's guilt and Ackley's self-loathing. Yet, and this is part of his tragedy, he is an impotent saint, unable either to redeem the fallen or to prevent their fall.

If the world of Holden's school was a muted purgatory, the world of his New York hotel is an insistent Hell. The window of his room provides him with a view of the other rooms in the hotel. In one, he sees a man dress himself in women's clothes, and in another, a man and woman who delight (sexually) in squirting water at each other from their mouths. This is the "real" world, with its respectable shade lifted, which fascinates and seduces Holden by its prurience. Having lost the sense of his innocence, he seeks sexual initiation as a means of redemption. His attraction to older women suggests that his quest for a woman is really a search for a mother whose love will protect him against the corrupt world as well as initiate him into it. Where the father-quest is a search for wisdom and spirit (God), the mother-quest is a search not for sex but ultimately for Love. They are different manifestations, one intellectual, the other physical, of the same spiritual quest. His search for sexual experience, Salinger indicates, is the only love alternative left Holden after he loses Jane. Once the possibility of innocent love ceases to exist, sexual love seems the next best thing, a necessary compensation for the loss of the first. However, Holden is only mildly disappointed when he is unable to arrange a date with a reputedly promiscuous girl whose telephone number he has inherited from a Princeton acquaintance. For all his avowed "sexiness," he is an innocent, and his innocence-impelled fear dampens his desire. Though the women he meets are by and large less disappointing than the men, they too fail Holden and intensify his despair. That they are not as good as he would like them to be seems to him *his* fault, *his* responsibility, *his* failure.

If Jane represents sacred love profaned, the prostitute who comes to Holden's room represents profane love unprofaned. After he has agreed to have her come to his room (the elevator operator, Maurice, is go-between), he refuses to make love to her once she is there. The scene is a crucial one in defining Holden's nontraditional sainthood. Holden refuses the prostitute not because of moral principle, but because the condition of her existence (she is about Holden's age and a kind of lost-innocent) depresses him.

> I took her dress over to the closet and hung it up for her. It was funny. It made me feel sort of sad when I hung it up. I thought of her going in a store and buying it, and nobody in the store knowing she was a prostitute and all. The salesman probably just thought she was a regular girl when she bought it. It made me feel sad as hell—I don't know why exactly.

He would save her if he could, but she is far too fallen for any catcher in the rye. But as child-saint, Holden is quixotic. In not sleeping with her, he means to protect her innocence, not his own; he is spiritually, hence physically, unable to be a party to her further degradation. The consequences are ironic. Holden as a saint refuses to victimize the prostitute, but he is victimized by the girl and her accomplice, Maurice. Though Holden has paid the girl without using her, Maurice beats Holden and extorts an additional five dollars from him. This episode is a more intense recapitulation of the Stradlater experience. In both cases Holden is punished for his innocence. If the hotel is a symbolic Hell, Maurice, as far as Holden is concerned, is its chief devil. In offering Holden the girl and then humiliating him for not accepting his expensive gift, Maurice is another of Holden's evil fathers.

Holden Suffers an Emotional Breakdown

After disillusionment with Antolini, who is the most destructive of Holden's fathers because he is seemingly the most benevolent, Holden suffers an emotional breakdown. His flight from Antolini's house, like his previous flights from school and from the hotel, is an attempt to escape evil. The three are parallel experiences, except that Holden is less sure of the justness of his third flight and wonders if he has not misjudged his otherwise sympathetic teacher.

> And the more I thought about it, the more depressed I got. I mean I started thinking maybe I *should've* gone back to his house. Maybe he *was* only patting my head just for the hell of it. The more I thought about it, though, the more depressed and screwed up about it I got.

The ambivalence of his response racks him. If he has misjudged Antolini, he has wronged not only his teacher, but he has wronged himself as well; he, not Antolini, has been guilty of corruption. Consequently, he suffers both for Antolini and for himself. Holden's guilt-ridden despair manifests itself in nausea and in an intense sense of physical ill-being, as if he carries the whole awful corruption of the city inside him. Walking aimlessly through the Christmas-decorated city, Holden experiences "the terrible, terrible fall" that Antolini had prophesied for him.

> Every time I came to the end of a block and stepped off the goddam curb, I had this feeling that I'd never get to the other side of the street. I thought I'd go down, down, down, and nobody'd ever see me again. Boy, did it scare me. You can't imagine. I started sweating like a bastard—my whole shirt and underwear and everything. . . . Every time I'd get to the end of a block I'd make believe I was talking to my brother Allie. I'd say to him, "Allie, don't let me disappear. Allie, don't let me disappear. Allie, don't let me disappear. Please, Allie." And then when I'd reach the other side of the street without disappearing, I'd *thank* him.

Like Franny's prayer to Jesus in one of Salinger's later stories, Holden's prayer to Allie is not so much an act of anguish as an act of love, though it is in part both. Trapped in an interior hell, Holden seeks redemption, not by formal appeal to God or Jesus, who have in the Christmas season been falsified and commercialized, but by praying to his saint-brother who in his goodness had God in him.

Like so many heroes of contemporary fiction—[Wright] Morris' Boyd [in *The Field of Vision* and *Ceremony in Lone Tree*], [Ralph] Ellison's Invisible Man [in *Invisible Man*], [Bernard] Malamud's Frank [in *The Assistant*], Salinger's Seymour—Holden is an impotent savior. Because he can neither save his evil world nor live in it as it is, he retreats into fantasy—into childhood. He decides to become a deaf-mute, to live alone in an isolated cabin, to commit a kind of symbolic suicide. It is an unrealizable fantasy, but a death wish nevertheless. However, Holden's social conscience forces him out of spiritual retirement. When he discovers an obscenity scrawled on one of the walls of Phoebe's school, he rubs it out with his hand to protect the innocence of the children. For the moment he is a successful catcher in the rye. But then he discovers another such notice, "*scratched* on, with a knife or something," and then another. He realizes that he cannot possibly erase all the scribbled obscenities in the world, that he cannot catch all the children, that evil is ineradicable.

This is the final disillusionment. Dizzy with his terrible awareness, Holden insults Phoebe when she insists on running away with him. In his vision of despair, he sees Phoebe's irrevocable doom as well as his own, and for a moment he hates her as he hates himself—as he hates the world. Once he has hurt her, however, he realizes the commitment that his love for her imposes on him; if he is to assuage her pain, he must continue to live in the world. When she kisses him as a token of forgiveness and love and, as if in consequence, it begins to rain, Holden, bathed by the rain, is purified—in a sense, redeemed.

Innocence Is the Way to Redemption

A too literal reading of Holden's divulgence that he is telling the story from some kind of rest home has led to a misinterpretation of the end of the novel. Holden is always less insane than his world. The last scene, in which Holden, suffused with happiness, sits in the rain and watches Phoebe ride on the merry-go-round, is indicative not of his crack-up, as has been assumed, but of his redemption. Whereas all the adults in his world have failed him (and he, a butter-fingered catcher in the rye, has failed them), a ten-year-old girl saves him—becomes his catcher. Love is the redemptive grace. Phoebe replaces Jane, the loss of whom had initiated Holden's despair, flight, and quest for experience as salvation. Holden's pure communion with Phoebe may be construed as a reversion to childlike innocence, but this is the only way to redemption in Salinger's world—there is no other good. Innocence is all. Love is innocence.

The last scene, with Holden drenched in Scott Fitzgerald's all-absolving rain, seems unashamedly sentimental. [At the graveside service in Fitzgerald's *Great Gatsby*, someone says, "Blessed are the dead that the rain falls on."] Certainly Salinger overstates the spiritually curative powers of children; innocence can be destructive as well as redemptive. Yet Salinger's view of the universe, in which all adults (even the most apparently decent) are corrupt and consequently destructive, is bleak and somewhat terrifying. Since growing up in the real world is tragic, in Salinger's ideal world time must be stopped to prevent the loss of childhood, to salvage the remnants of innocence. At one point in the novel, Holden wishes that life were as changeless and pure as the exhibitions under glass cases in the Museum of Natural History. This explains, in part, Holden's ecstasy in the rain at the close of the novel. In watching Phoebe go round and round on the carrousel, in effect going nowhere, he sees her in the timeless continuum of art on the verge of changing, yet unchanging, forever safe, forever loving, forever innocent.

Holden Caulfield Is Depressed by the World and by His Own Failings

Ihab Hassan

Ihab Hassan is Vilas Research Professor of English and Comparative Literature at the University of Wisconsin-Milwaukee and the author of more than fifteen books and numerous articles on literary criticism. This essay was reprinted from Radical Innocence, *which is considered one of the seminal works on the contemporary American novel.*

Ihab Hassan claims that Salinger has fashioned a new American Dream in The Catcher in the Rye. *Salinger has captured, with humor and grace, the quest of the adolescent to shed innocence and arrive at truth. However, Hassan writes, Holden Caulfield is thwarted in his quest. He is depressed by the phoniness of the world around him and filled with self-disgust at his own failings.*

[Salinger] has written some of the best fiction of our time. His voice is genuine, new, and startlingly uneven. In his work we find no showy or covert gesture in the direction of Symbolism or Naturalism, Gothic design or Freudian chiaroscuro [psychological struggles of light against dark]; and indeed there was a time when we were unsure whether his intentions came closer to those of [Henry] Fielding or [Ronald] Firbank, [Mark] Twain or [Anton] Chekov. If close to anything, Salinger's intentions are probably more in keeping with [F. Scott] Fitzgerald's idea of self-created innocence and [Ring] Lardner's biting renderings of corruption, with the spiritual assumptions of Martin Buber, and, more recently, with those of primitive Christianity and Zen. Yet to speak of his uniqueness in these terms is simply to indulge in the small talk of criticism. We are more anxious, nowadays, to discover the opportunities of literary significance, the conditions of heresy, and protocols of formal excellence. We question *Kitsch* [vulgar or tawdry] and middle-brow art to the extent that we consume it in prodigious quantities, and are adversely disposed to any serious work that carries the aura of either. It is in response to this line of criticism that the work of Salinger proves itself to be seriously engaged by a current and a traditional aspect of reality in America.

The New American Dream

The traditional aspect wears no elaborate disguise. It is the new look of the American Dream, specifically dramatized by the encounter between a vision of innocence and the reality of guilt, between the forms love and power have tended to assume in America. The natural locus of that conflict in the work of Salinger is childhood and adolescence. In them the counterplay of hope and despair, truth and mendacity, participation and withdrawal, commands a full range of comic, that is ambivalent, reference: it is the old story of the self against the world in outlines blurred by a mass society. To say as [literary critic Leslie] Fiedler does that the "images of childhood and adolescence haunt our greatest works as an unintended symbolic confession of the inadequacy we sense but cannot remedy" is to view a profound truth in a partial perspective. Nostalgia . . . is the result of our compulsion to reenact the story of the American fall. We do not always resist it well. But nostalgia, when it is known to itself, has its ironic and artistic uses. The retreat to childhood is not simply an escape; it is also a criticism, an affirmation of values which, for better or worse, we still cherish; and the need for adolescent disaffiliation, the refusal of initiation, expresses the need to reconceive American reality.

Yet it is hard for some critics to recognize that no act of denial in Salinger's work is without some dramatic and social correlative, which is more than we can generally say of equally serious novelists writing today. The urban, suburban, and ex-urban society which circumscribes Salinger's child and adolescent characters—the white dinner, not black leather, jacket circle—is usually well specified. About that society we have recently learned a good deal. We know that it exhibits a sad decay of genuine sensibility and even of simple truth. There are, no doubt, many opportunities of significant action still left in it, and we are justified in requesting our best writers to discover them. But the nature of action is such that its results are seldom commensurate with its motives. And the reverse is no less true. The anger of a child confronted for the first time with the force of anti-Semitism, the spirit of an adolescent who dons a red hunting cap in New York City, the tender cruelty of a woman, who is bereaved of her lover, toward her child, even the suicide of a misfit genius, can suggest possibilities of action which we hastily reject in favor of a mechanical gesture at the polling booth. Social realities are no doubt repressed in the work of Salinger—note how gingerly he handles his Jews—and this puts a limit on the total significance we can accord to it. Yet it is by what an author manages to *dramatize* that we must finally judge him.

The Conflict Between the Vulgarian and Outsider

The dramatic conflict which so many of Salinger's stories present obviously does not lend itself to sociological classification. It is more loving and particular, and it partakes of situations that have been traditionally available to literature. The conflict, however, suggests a certain polarity between what might be called, with all due exaggeration, the Assertive Vulgarian and the Responsive Outsider. Both types recur with sufficient frequency to warrant the distinction, and their interplay defines much that is most central to Salinger's fiction. The Vulgarian, who carries the burden of squalor, stands for all that is crude, venal, self-absorbed, and sequacious [unthinkingly subservient] in our culture. He has no access to knowledge or feeling or beauty, which makes him all the more invulnerable, and his relationship to the world is largely predicated by [Martin] Buber's I-It dyad. He or she can be rich or poor: Evelyn Cooney in "Elaine," Mrs. Ford and the Croftses in "The Inverted Forest," Sandra and Mrs. Snell in "Down at the Dinghy," Joanie in "Pretty Mouth and Green My Eyes," The Matron of Honor in "Raise High the Roof Beam, Carpenters," Maurice, Stradlater, or any number of others in *The Catcher in the Rye*. These, in a sense, are Spiritual Tramps, as Seymour called his wife in "A Perfect Day for Banana Fish," though he might have better said it of her mother. The Outsider, on the other hand, carries the burden of love. The burden makes of him sometimes a victim, and sometimes a scapegoat saint. His life is like "a great inverted forest/with all foliage underground" [as written in Salinger's "The Inverted Forest"]. It is a quick, generous, and responsive life, somehow preserved against hardness and corruption, and always attempting to reach out from its isolation in accordance with Buber's I-Thou dyad. Often there is something in the situation of the Outsider to isolate him, to set him off, however slightly, from the rest of mankind. He might be a child or an adolescent, might wear glasses or appear disfigured, might be Jewish, though seldom is he as crippled or exotic as the characters of [Truman] Capote and [Carson] McCullers often are. His ultimate defense, as [Rainer Maria] Rilke, to whom Salinger refers, put it, is defenselessness. Raymond Ford, Boo Boo Tannenbaum (Glass) and her son, Lionel, Seymour and other members of the Glass family, Holden and Phoebe, in the previous stories, are examples of that type.

The response of these outsiders and victims to the dull or angry world about them is not simply one of withdrawal: it

A worn paperback copy of J.D. Salinger's The Catcher in the Rye. © Martin Heitner/ Superstock.

often takes the form of a strange, quixotic gesture. The gesture, one feels sure, is the bright metaphor of Salinger's sensibility, the center from which meaning drives, and ultimately the reach of his commitment to past innocence and current guilt. It is a gesture at once of pure expression and of expectation, of protest and prayer, of aesthetic form and spiritual content—as [poet and critic R.P.] Blackmur would say, it is behavior that sings. There is often something prodigal and spontaneous about it, something humorous or whimsical, something that disrupts our habits of gray acquiescence and revives our faith in the willingness of the human spirit. But above all, it gives of itself as only a *religious* gesture can. In another age, [Miguel de] Cervantes endowed Don Quixote with the capacity to perform it, and so did Twain and Fitzgerald endow their best creations. For the gesture, after all, has an unmistakably American flourish. The quest of American adolescents, as we saw, has always been for an idea of truth. It is this very idea of truth that the quixotic gesture is constantly seeking to embody. The embodiment is style in action: the twist and tang, the stammering and improvisations, the glint and humor of Salinger's language. . . .

Holden Caulfield Is a Hero in Flight from Hypocrisy

The Catcher in the Rye inevitably stands out as Salinger's only novel to date. As a "neo-picaresque," the book shows itself to be concerned far less with the education or initiation of an adolescent than with a dramatic exposure of the manner in which ideals are denied access to our lives and of the modes which mendacity assumes in our urban culture. The moving, even stabbing, qualities of the novel derive, to some extent, from Salinger's refusal to adopt a satirical stance. The work, instead, confirms the saving grace of vulnerability; its protest, debunking, and indictments presuppose a willing responsiveness on the part of its hero.

On the surface, Holden Caulfield is Salinger's typical quixotic hero in search, once again, of the simple truth. Actually,

Holden is in flight from mendacity rather than in search of truth, and his sensitivity to the failures of the world is compounded with his self-disgust. In comparison with his dear, dead brother, Allie, a kind of redheaded saint who united intelligence and compassion as no other member of the family could, setting for all a standard of performance which they try to recapture, Holden seems intolerant, perhaps even harsh. The controlling mood of the novel—and it is so consistent as to be a principle of unity—is one of acute depression always on the point of breaking loose. But despair and depression are kept, throughout, in check by Holden's remarkable lack of self-interest, a quality of self-heedlessness which is nearly saintly, and by his capacity to invoke his adolescent imagination, to "horse around," when he is most likely to go to pot. These contrary pressures keep the actions of the novel in tension and keep the theme of sentimental disenchantment on the stretch; and they are sustained by a style of versatile humor.

The action begins at a prep school from which Holden has flunked out, and continues in various parts of Manhattan; it covers some three days of the Christmas season. The big city, decked out in holiday splendor and gaudiness, is nevertheless unprepared for Holden's naked vision, and it seldom yields any occasions of peace, charity, or even genuine merriment. From the moment Holden leaves Pencey behind, leaves its Stradlaters and Ackleys, its oafs, creeps, and hypocrites, and dons his red hunting cap—why not, it's a mad world, isn't it?—we know that we are on to an adventure of pure self-expression, if not self-discovery.

In New York, it is once again the same story of creeps and hypocrites revealed in larger perspective. We hardly need to recapitulate the crowded incidents of the novel to see that Holden is motivated by a compelling desire to commune and communicate, a desire constantly thwarted by the phoniness, indifference, and vulgarity that surround him. He resents the conditions which force upon him the burden of rejection. In protest against these conditions, he has devised a curious game of play-acting, of harmless and gratuitous lying, which is his way of coming to terms with a blistered sensibility, and of affirming his values of truth and imagination. But above all, he is continually performing the quixotic gesture. Thus he socks Stradlater, who is twice his weight, because he suspects the latter of having seduced [Jane] Gallagher, without any consideration of the fact that she is the kind of girl to keep all her kings, at checkers, in the back row. He gives money away to nuns. He can read a child's notebook all day and night. He furiously rubs out obscenities from the walls of schools. And when Phoebe asks him very seriously what he would like to be, he muses on Robert Burns's song, "If a body meet a body coming through the rye," which he had heard a kid hum in the street, and answers back: ". . . I keep picturing all these kids playing some game in this big field of rye and all. Thousands of little kids, and nobody's around—nobody big, I mean—except me. And I'm standing on the edge of some crazy cliff. . . . That's all I'd do all day. I'd just be the catcher in the rye and all. I know it's crazy. . . ."

Holden Caulfield Is a Biased, Unstable Narrator

A closer look at *The Catcher in the Rye* might allow us to separate its real from imaginary failings. Mr. Aldridge, for instance, taking his cue perhaps from Phoebe's comment to her brother, "You don't like *any*thing that's happening," has recently observed—Maxwell Geismar makes exactly the same point—that Holden "has objects for his contempt but no objects other than his sister for his love." It is true that Holden has *more* objects for his contempt than his love—this is the expense of his idealism and the price of his rebellion. But it is impossible to overlook his various degrees of affection for Allie, his dead brother, for James Castle, the boy who was killed because he wouldn't retract a statement he thought true, for the kettle drummer at Radio City, the nuns at the lunch counter, the kid humming the title song, or even the ducks in the park, without missing something of Holden's principal commitments. And his answer to Phoebe, "People never think anything is anything *really*. I'm getting goddam sick of it," may do for those who find these commitments rather slim. Nor can we disallow the feeling of pity which often modifies Holden's scorn, his pity for Ackley and the girls in the Lavender Room, or his confession to Antolini that he can hate people only part of the time, and that he quickly misses those whom he may have once hated. Holden, of course, is not in the least cynical; nor is he blind except to part of the truth which he can otherwise entertain so steadily. Still, there are those who feel that the novel accords no recognition to its hero, and that it fails to enlist our sense of tragedy. The lack of recognition, the avoidance of conversion and initiation, is almost as inherent in the structure of the novel as it is consonant with the bias of the American novel of adolescence. The action of the book is recollected by Holden who is out West recuperating from his illness, and Holden only chooses to tell us "about this madman stuff that happened to me around last Christmas"—nothing more. He refuses to relate incidents to his past or to his character, and he refuses to draw any conclusions from his experience: "If you want to know the truth, I don't *know* what I think about it. . . . About all I know is, I sort of *miss* everybody I told about. Even old Stradlater and Ackley, for instance. . . . Don't ever tell anybody anything. If you do, you start missing everybody." This is an embarrassed testament of love, full of unresolved ambiguities, the only lyrical and undramatic recognition the novel can afford. The partial blindness of Holden, which has been correctly attributed to Holden's juvenile impatience with the reality of compromise, is made more serious by Salinger's failure to modify Holden's point of view by any other. In *Joseph Andrews* [by

Henry Fielding], for instance, the innocence of Adams is constantly criticized by the tone of the book and the nature of its comic incidents. There is also some danger that we may be too easily disarmed by the confessional candor of Salinger's novel. When Holden says time and time again, "I swear to God I'm crazy," the danger is equally great in taking Holden at his word as in totally discounting his claim. Holden does succeed in making us perceive that the world is crazy, but his vision is also a function of his own adolescent instability, and the vision, we must admit, is more narrow and biased than that of Huck Finn, Parson Adams, or Don Quixote. It is this narrowness that limits the comic effects of the work. Funny it is without any doubt, and in a fashion that has been long absent from American fiction. But we must recall that true comedy is informed by the spirit of compromise, not intransigence. Huck Finn and Augie March [protagonist of Saul Bellow's *The Adventures of Augie March*] are both, in this sense, closer to the assumptions of comedy than Holden Caulfield. This once understood, we can see how *The Catcher in the Rye* is *both* a funny and terrifying work—traditional distinctions of modes have broken down in our time—a work full of pathos in the original sense of the word. But suffering is a subjective thing, and the novel's sly insistence on suffering makes it a more subjective work than the two novels which relate the adventures of Huck Finn and Augie March. Adventure is precisely what Holden does not endure; his sallies into the world are feigned; his sacrificial burden, carried with whimsey and sardonic defiance, determines his fate. The fate is that of the American rebel-victim. . . .

Salinger Is an American Poet

But from the early search for innocence to the later testament of love, from the slick adequacy of his earlier style to the tense lyrical form of his later, if not latest, stories, Salinger has kept faith with the redeeming powers of outrage and compassion.

His faith in these has not always allowed him to reconcile their shifting focus or to create the forms of dramatic permanence. When reconciliation is granted, when the rare, quixotic gesture, striking through, becomes the form of fiction, incarnate and ineluctable, we see Salinger at last for what he is: an American poet, his thin and intelligent face all but lost among the countless faces of the modern city, his vision, forever lonely and responsive, troubled by the dream of innocence and riddled by the presence both of love and of squalor. What saves Salinger's vision from sentimentality is the knowledge that no man can give an object more tenderness than God accords to it. His heroes, children, adolescents, or adult victims to the affluence of their own spirit, play upon our nostalgia for a mythic American past. They also manage to raise nostalgia to the condition of hope.

Holden Caulfield Suffers from Unresolved Sexual Conflict

Duane Edwards

Duane Edwards taught at Fairleigh Dickinson University.

Duane Edwards contends that critics who admire Holden Caulfield fail to recognize that he himself is a phony who does not live up to the ideals he values. The roots of Holden's problems, asserts Edwards, are in his unresolved sexual conflicts, specifically his latent homosexual tendencies. His sexual confusion is understandable, given his unfortunate family situation with distant parents, and it makes him a sympathetic, likable character. However, Edwards argues, because Holden refuses to take responsibility for his actions, he will remain ill.

Salinger's admirers have responded in a variety of ways to *The Catcher in the Rye*, but most have something in common: they idealize Holden. In order to do so, they play down the seriousness of his ambivalence, exhibitionism, and voyeurism and assign the blame for his severe depression entirely to society, to the world of perverts and bums and phonies. Failing to respond to the first person narrator as ironic, they assume that Holden should be taken at his word; that he is right and the world wrong; that there is a sharp dichotomy between Holden and the world he loathes. . . .

What these writers ignore is that Holden shares in the phoniness he loathes; that he lives by his unconscious needs and not the values he espouses; that he withdraws from rather than faces the challenge of personal relationships.

Duane Edwards, "Holden Caulfield: Don't Ever Tell Anybody Anything," *English Literary History*, vol. 44, Fall 1977, pp. 556–567. Copyright © 1977 The Johns Hopkins University Press. Reproduced by permission.

Holden Caulfield Is a Phony Himself

It's not difficult to understand why readers have ignored, or have failed to perceive, Holden's grave deficiencies as a person. After all, he is very appealing—on the surface. He genuinely appreciates brief and isolated instances of kindness and accurately pinpoints phoniness in both high and low places; he is witty and his love for Phoebe is touching. But he himself is a phony at times, and he has virtually no self-awareness. Furthermore, he has no intention of gaining self-awareness. Offered good advice by the psychoanalyst Wilhelm Stekel (through Mr. Antolini), he becomes "so damned *tired* all of a sudden" and is unable to concentrate. Confronted with the charge that he cannot name one "thing" he likes "a lot," he again cannot "concentrate too hot." Of course he can't; he's too busy repressing the truth. So he rambles on about two nuns he met briefly and will never see again, and he tries to convince Phoebe—and himself—that he likes James Castle, a boy who is dead. But he cannot name one *living* person, or even one occupation, that he likes. Nevertheless, he believes he is a lover of people in general because he wants to be the catcher in the rye.

When Holden says that he wants to be the catcher in the rye, he reveals a great deal about himself—a great deal more than he knows. He reveals that he does not seriously want to learn about himself. He simply won't make the effort. After all, he hasn't bothered to read Burns's poem; he isn't even able to quote accurately the one line he heard a small boy recite; he doesn't know that Burns's narrator contemplates kissing the "body" he meets in the rye field. So when Holden changes the word "meet" to "catch" and talks not of love but of potential death (falling off a cliff), he reveals his willingness to distort the truth by ignoring—or even changing—the facts. He also reveals his use of displacement: he substitutes one response for another. He focuses on danger and potential death instead of love and a personal relationship. Ultimately, he reveals his unreliability as the narrator of his own life's story.

Fortunately, the fact that Holden distorts doesn't matter to anyone concerned with the *significance* of the events and dialogue recorded in *The Catcher in the Rye*. Like the psychoanalyst analyzing a dream, the reader can analyze what matters most: the distortions. What emerges from this analysis is an awareness that Salinger's narrator is ironic: he doesn't understand (or know) himself, but he unwittingly lets the reader know what he is like. In fact, he does so at the very beginning of the novel when he promises to give the reader "none of that David Copperfield crap" about his "lousy childhood." Normally, such a statement would be innocent and unrevealing, but Holden isn't "normal": he's a severely depressed adolescent telling the story of his youth while in a mental institution. He is, by his own admission, sick. So his refusal to talk about the incidents of his childhood signifies that he will remain ill, as does his chilling advice, "Don't ever tell anybody anything," at the end of the novel.

Elsewhere in the novel there is evidence that Holden will remain ill because he refuses to assume responsibility for his own actions. For example, when he is "the goddam manager of the fencing team," he leaves the "foils and equipment and stuff" on the subway. Although he admits that he left them there, he hastens to add: "It wasn't all my fault." Here and elsewhere he simply will not or can not let his mind rest without ambivalence or qualification on a conclusion.

Ambivalence is, in fact, characteristic of Holden and the surest evidence of his mental instability. If he loathes what he loves and does so intensely, he is by no means well. He is also not what he and many readers assume he is: an anti-establishment figure whose disgust is directed entirely at other people. . . .

Holden Caulfield Is Unable to Relate to Females

What is Holden's problem? Whatever it is in specific form, it's reflected in his inability to relate sexually to females. Holden himself suggests this when he says, "My sex life stinks." But even when he speaks the truth he fools himself: he believes that he cannot "get really sexy" with girls he doesn't like a lot whereas, in reality, he cannot get sexy with a girl he does like. In fact, what he likes about Jane Gallagher is that a relationship with her will not go beyond the hand-holding stage. In his other attempts to establish connections with girls or women, he fails sexually and, in fact, deliberately avoids both affection and serious sexual advances. He kisses Sally Hayes—but in a cab where the relationship cannot go beyond "horsing around." He consents to have a prostitute sent to his hotel room but asks her to stop when she starts "getting funny. Crude and all," that is, when she proceeds from words to action. Aroused by watching the "perverts" in the hotel, he does call up Faith Cavendish, a woman he has never seen, but at an impossibly late hour and so ensures that she will refuse his request for a date. Clearly, Holden has a problem with females.

This problem is reflected in his response to Mercutio in *Romeo and Juliet*. Acting in character, Holden identifies with Mercutio, the character in the play he has most in common with. As [critic Carl F.] Strauch has pointed out, both Holden and Mercutio are associated with foils. But the two have much more in common than weapons. To begin with, Mercutio assigns the role of lover to Romeo just as Holden assigns the role of lover to Stradlater. Then, too, both young men ramble on when they talk. Mr. Antolini reminds us that this is true of Holden; Romeo calls Mercutio's long speech "nothing" and Mercutio himself admits that he talks of "dreams / Which are the children of an idle brain, / Begot of nothing but vain fantasy." Finally, both Mercutio and Holden like to "horse around." Holden does so repeatedly; Mercutio does so even when he's dying.

What these two characters have in common at the level of speech and overt behavior reveals how they are alike in subtler ways. For example, both talk about, but do not engage in, sexual love. Both are more enamoured of words than facts. Both are victims—from Holden's point of view. Mercutio is the victim of the Capulets and of Romeo's desire to live at peace in the world; Holden sees himself as the victim of snobs, perverts, and phonies. Since Holden identifies with victims in general and, in fact, projects his suffering onto them, he has sympathy for the ducks in Central Park, for Selma Thurmer, and for the lunatic in *Mark V*. It follows logically that he likes Mercutio.

It also follows logically that he did not like "Romeo too much after Mercutio gets stabbed." Clearly, Romeo is the antithesis of both Mercutio and Holden. He is passionate; he speaks without irony; he goes to bed with Juliet. He is by no means sexually shy although he, like Holden, is very young. In contrast, Holden is sexually shy; paradoxically, he also has an exhibitionistic attitude, that is, he has a *need* to attract attention to himself by attempting "to amuse, to stir, or to shock others." Acting on this need, he performs for Stradlater in the men's room; he pretends to have a bullet in his stomach; performing for Ackley, he pulls his hunting hat over his eyes and says in a hoarse voice, "I think I'm going blind"; wears a red hunting cap in the streets of New York. He even calls himself an exhibitionist to attract attention to himself.

It's true that each of these examples of exhibitionism is, in itself, both harmless and normal, especially for a boy of Holden's age. (Holden himself would say that he was simply "horsing around.") But Holden has a need to show off, and he has more serious problems eventually. After all, he does end up in a mental institution. Consequently, his exhibitionistic attitude serves as a clue to his state of mind; it also helps to explain why Holden "got sick and all." Since he himself won't tell us, this clue is especially important.

Holden Is a Voyeur

Other important clues to Holden's problem are included in Chapter 25, the chapter following Holden's flight from Mr. Antolini and preceding the one-page concluding chapter which reveals that Holden is in a mental institution. Near the beginning of Chapter 25, Holden's mental breakdown (which is not recorded in the novel) is anticipated: Holden has a headache and feels "more depressed than [he] ever was in [his] whole life." He also has the desire to catch what he assumes is "some perverty bum that'd sneaked in the school late at night to take a leak or something and then wrote [an obscenity] on the wall." And, finally, he notices—and comments on—a little boy who "had his pants open." . . .

[A] subjectivity and tendency to distort explains a great deal about Holden. Specifically, it explains his interest in the "perverty bum" and the little boy whose pants are unbuttoned. Both appeal to him because of his voyeuristic tendencies.

That Holden has voyeuristic tendencies should surprise no one. He himself admits that he finds it "sort of fascinating to watch" bizarre sexual activity through his hotel window. Besides, [as Sigmund Freud wrote] anyone "who in the unconscious is an exhibitionist is at the same time a voyeur" in psychoanalytic terms. So it is not surprising that Holden is interested in the "perverty bum" and the little boy. What is surprising is the degree of his response. In the first instance he responds with extreme hostility; he wants to catch the bum urinating and/or writing on the wall (Holden is a bit ambiguous here) and "smash his head on the stone steps till he was good and goddam dead and bloody." In the second instance he responds with extreme concern and embarrassment; he says the boy's behavior "killed" him and adds that he wanted to laugh when the boy buttoned his pants without going behind a post, but he didn't dare to; he was afraid he'd "feel like vomiting again."

What is happening is that looking is becoming a perversion for Holden: it is beginning to be concentrated on the genitals and associated with the function of excretion. It also does not prepare for the normal sexual act and is the logical, although not "normal," outgrowth of his sexual shyness, of his reluctance to go beyond holding hands. It also follows quite naturally from the fact that Holden is sexually ambivalent; he hasn't lost interest in females and cannot acknowledge his sexual interest in males.

Homosexuality in *Catcher*

Most critics writing about homosexuality in *The Catcher in the Rye* assume that Holden is the victim of homosexuals, but there is a great deal of evidence to the contrary. To begin with, Holden fails to complete most of his phone calls to females, but he easily completes phone calls to two homosexuals: Mr. Antolini and Carl Luce. Secondly, *he* seeks *them* out; he is the aggressor if there is one. In fact, his first two remarks to Luce reveal his unconscious desire to make sexual contact with his former Student Adviser. "Hey, I got a flit for you," he says first of all, and then asks him, "How's your sex life?" Thirdly, Salinger links Holden to the two homosexuals by letting the reader know (through the narration) that all three of them respond sexually to older women: Luce is dating a woman in her late thirties; Antolini is married to a woman who "looked pretty old and all"; Holden responds sexually to Ernest Morrow's mother. But nothing reveals more about Holden's relationship to homosexuals than his response when he wakes up in the middle of the night in Mr. Antolini's house. Consider his exact words:

I woke up all of a sudden. I don't know what time it was or anything, but I woke up. I felt something on my head, some guy's hand. Boy, it really scared hell out of me. What it was, it was Mr. Antolini's hand. What he was doing was, he was sitting on the floor right next to the couch, in the dark and all, and he was sort of petting me or patting me on the goddam head.

Since Holden tells us that Antolini is there in the dark touching him, we have to assume this is true; there is nothing to negate or contradict or undercut this statement. But what Antolini's intention was we cannot know since even Holden is confused. Antolini was patting *or* petting him, Holden says. But the difference between patting and petting is great: we pat children and pet lovers. Furthermore, nothing that Holden says about Antolini's response to Holden's wild flight in the night suggests that Antolini is guilty of making a sexual advance. Besides, what matters most of all in this incident is Holden's distortion of experience, specifically, his overreaction. Even if Antolini did make an improper move, Holden is safe: Mrs. Antolini is in the adjoining room; Antolini is by no means aggressive; and Antolini has agreed to go to bed.

Why, then, does Holden respond so violently? Why is he sweating and ill when he leaves the house? The answer is that he is projecting his desire for homosexual expression onto Antolini. (This does not mean that Holden is himself a homosexual but that he has not yet made a sexual choice.) In the passage cited above, this is evident. Holden assumes that "some guy's hand" is on his head before he can identify Mr. Antolini or identify the hand as his. Furthermore, in this same scene he acknowledges, as the ironic narrator, that he inspires such behavior. He says, first of all, that perverts are "always being perverty when *I'm* around" and emphasizes that this "kind of stuff's happened to me about twenty times since I was a kid." Naturally. He is attracted to—and attracts—homosexuals.

Unfortunately, Holden isn't conscious of this. In fact, he works hard to repress all knowledge of his latent desires. To begin with, he doesn't seem to be conscious of the significance of his remarks to Carl Luce in the bar even though he admits that he "used to think" Luce was "sort of flitty." But the patting (or petting) incident is more overt and threatens to make Holden conscious of his latent homosexual desires. He reacts by becoming ill. He has a headache, becomes anxious and depressed, has sore eyes, experiences a mild form of hypochondria when he says he has "lousy hormones" and cancer, and wishes to negate his identity by "going out West" where nobody would know him. But, most important of all, he wants to be unable to hear or speak; he wants to be a deaf mute who marries and lives in isolation with a beautiful deaf mute girl. In other words, Holden wants to live apart from men and wants to be unable to hear or speak anything. In expressing this Holden expresses his wish to have no reminders through speech or action of his unresolved sexual conflict.

Holden's Family Situation

It shouldn't be surprising that Holden has severe sexual conflicts: his family situation is far from ideal. The father barely exists as far as Holden and Phoebe are concerned, and the mother is not emotionally involved in the lives of her children. This is revealed in the scene in which the Caulfields return from a party. First of all, they are indifferent to Phoebe. Although she is still a child, they have left her home alone. When they do return home late at night, only Mrs. Caulfield bothers to look in on her daughter. But she is by no means greatly concerned. She doesn't object seriously to what she assumes is smoke from a cigarette Phoebe has been smoking; she moves randomly and nervously (like Holden) from one subject to another, including Holden's return from school; she fails to react to Phoebe's statement that she couldn't sleep. In brief, she is a mother incapable of affection.

Meanwhile, the father has gone into another room without bothering to inquire about Phoebe. Since Phoebe has said that he will not attend her Christmas pageant, it's safe to assume that he is generally absent from his children's lives. He is the aloof father whose inaccessibility makes it impossible for his son to identify with him and thus to develop "normally."

But he does have a connection with Holden: he punishes him. Confirming this, Phoebe says repeatedly that Mr. Caulfield will "kill" Holden, and Holden himself acknowledges that "it would've been very unpleasant and all" if his father had found him at home. Since Mr. Caulfield remains a vague and powerful figure, his effect on his son is inevitably exaggerated and debilitating. He joins forces with his wife to stifle and stunt his son's sexual development.

Holden Is Likable, but Ill

Because Holden's home situation is so unfortunate, it's easy to sympathize with him. It's even tempting to see the conclusion as affirmative. Besides, Holden is very appealing when he criticizes bums and phonies and perverts—so appealing that it's easy to forget that he's a bum, a phony (at times) and a potential pervert. And when he expresses his love for Phoebe, his hostility and egotism seem relatively unimportant. So it's tempting to see Holden as a person who doesn't need a psychoanalyst because he has gone beyond affirmation and denial. But at the end of the novel Holden is depressed and subdued. He has lost interest in life: he doesn't want to think about the past; he isn't interested in his future. When he tells D. B. that he doesn't know what to think about "all this stuff I just finished telling you about," he reveals that he is still confused. And when he says that he misses everybody—even Stradlater and Ackley and Maurice—he reveals that he is still sentimental. Although his sentimentality has often been sentimentalized as love, it is not love at all. It is a symptom of his inability to express his feelings easily and naturally.

Nevertheless, Holden is likable. He also deserves sympathy because, as William Faulkner has said, he "tried to join the human race and failed." But Faulkner is not quite accurate when he says that there was no human race for him to enter. Phoebe loves him; D. B. expresses an interest in him by visiting him in the mental institution; Mr. Antolini offers him shelter and good advice. Ultimately, people are as good to Holden as he is to them. So Holden should not be idealized. It may be true that he is [as Faulkner said at a conference at the University of Virginia in 1958] "more intelligent than some and more sensitive than most," but his response to his own experience results in deep depression and may have culminated in mania. Nor does Holden resist the establishment that makes it difficult for him to love and develop. His rebellion is all fantasy. He tells off no one—not even the prostitute or the phonies at Pencey. And his overt behavior is conventional except when he is acting out his exhibitionistic attitude. He doesn't become a recluse or a beatnik; instead, he returns home, enters an institution, and will *again* return to school in the fall.

He does have what Faulkner calls an "instinct" to love man, but this makes him a typical, rather than extraordinary, teenager. It's what causes him to want to join the human race.

What does make him extraordinary is his special ability to detect phoniness everywhere (except in himself). Of course it's unfair to emphasize, to the exclusion of everything else, that Holden shares in the phoniness he loathes. After all, Holden conforms to phoniness because he wants so badly to join the human race. But in doing so he makes it difficult for others like himself to find a human race to join.

Holden Caulfield's Problems Are Sexual

James Bryan

James Bryan is a literary critic.

James Bryan contends that Holden Caulfield's neurosis is caused by his fear that he is sexually attracted to his young sister, Phoebe. In this essay, Bryan analyzes Salinger's text to show double meanings and sexual references in the scenes between Holden and Phoebe. He concludes by saying that the process of narrating this story has been cathartic for Holden and that he has begun to gain control of his life.

M uch of the *Catcher* criticism has testified to Holden's acute moral and esthetic perceptions—his eye for beauty as well as "phoniness"—but the significance of his immaturity in intensifying these perceptions has not been sufficiently stressed nor explained. Precisely because this sixteen-year-old acts "like I'm about thirteen" and even "like I was only about twelve," he is hypersensitive to the exploitations and insensitivity of the postpubescent world and to the fragile innocence of children. A central rhythm of the narrative has Holden confronting adult callousness and retreating reflexively into thoughts and fantasies about children, child-like Jane Gallaghers, and especially his ten-year-old sister, Phoebe. These juxtapositions render both worlds more intensely and at the same time qualify Holden's judgments by showing that they are emotionally—or, as we shall see, neurotically—induced.

James Bryan, "The Psychological Structure of *The Catcher in the Rye*," *PMLA: Publications of the Modern Language Association of America*, vol. 89, October 1974, pp. 1065–1074. Copyright © 1974 by the Modern Language Association of America. Reprinted by permission of the Modern Language Association of America.

A Pattern of Sexual Aggression and Regression

While a fair number of critics have referred to Holden's "neurosis," none has accepted Salinger's invitation—proffered in the form of several key references to psychoanalysis—to participate in a full-fledged psychoanalytical reading. The narrative, after all, was written in a mental hospital with Holden under the care of a "psychoanalyst guy." One problem is that Holden tells us very little about "what my lousy childhood was like" or the event that may have brought on the trauma behind all of his problems: the death of a younger brother when Holden was thirteen. We know little more than that the family has been generally disrupted since and that Holden has not come to grips with life as he should have. Allie's death takes place outside the province of the narrative, but a valuable psychological study might still be made of the progression of Holden's breakdown—how he provokes fights in which he will be beaten, makes sexual advances he cannot carry through, and unconsciously alienates himself from many of the people he encounters. As a step toward psychological understanding, I shall consider certain manifestations of Holden's disturbances. An examination of the structure, scene construction, and suggestive imagery reveals a pattern of aggression and regression, largely sexual, which is suggested in the Pencey Prep section, acted out in the central part of the novel, and brought to a curious climax in the Phoebe chapters. . . .

Holden's Frantic Need to Save Phoebe from Himself

The expository sections of the novel dramatize Holden's problems as essentially sexual and moral. Yet most critical readings of the novel's ending either ignore these things or imply their absence by declaring that the resolution is "blunted" or else "humanly satisfying" while "artistically weak." Those critics who attest to a harmonious resolution generally do so on philosophical grounds, the effect being a divorce of theme from Holden's human situation. To deny a fused sexual and moral resolution of some sort in the closing emotional crescendo of the Phoebe section would, it seems to me, impugn the integrity of the novel.

I am suggesting that the urgency of Holden's compulsions, his messianic desire to guard innocence against adult corruption, for example, comes of a frantic need to save his sister from himself. It may be Phoebe's face that Holden unconsciously fears may be desecrated; hence the desire to protect Phoebe's face that compels his fascination with mummification. And it may be Phoebe who provokes his longing for stasis because he fears that she may be changed—perhaps at his own hand. Holden's association of sex with death surely points to some sexual guilt—possibly the fear that he or Phoebe or both may "die" if repressed desires are acted out.

I do not mean to imply that Holden's desires, if they are what I suggest, drive him inexorably to Phoebe's bed. The psychoanalytical axiom may here apply that a sister is often the first replacement of the mother as love object, and that normal maturation guides the boy from sister to other women. At this point in his life, Holden's sexuality is swaying precariously between reversion and maturation—a condition structurally dramatized throughout and alluded to in this early description:

> I was sixteen then, and I'm seventeen now, and sometimes I act like I'm about thirteen. It's really ironical, because I'm six foot two and a half and I have gray hair. I really do. The one side of my head—the right side—is full of millions of gray hairs. I've had them ever since I was a kid. And yet I still act sometimes like I was only about twelve. Everybody says that, especially my father. It's partly true, too, but it isn't *all* true. . . . Sometimes I act a lot older than I am—I really do—but people never notice it.

The narrator's overall perspective is thus mapped out: his present age representing some measure of maturity, and thirteen and twelve the vacillation that normally comes at puberty and that is so much more painful when it occurs as late as sixteen. This vacillation is somehow resolved in a climax beginning in Phoebe's bedroom (or rather the bedroom of D.B., the corrupt brother, where she sleeps) and ending at the carrousel after Holden has refused to let her run away with him. However one interprets the ending, it comes as a surprise which is dramatically appropriate precisely because it shocks Holden. . . .

Holden makes his way into the apartment furtively—ostensibly to keep his parents from learning that he had flunked out of school. Yet his guilt seems obsessive. "I really should've been a crook," he says after telling the elevator operator that he was visiting the "Dicksteins" who live next door, that he has to wait for them in their hallway because he has a "bad leg," causing him to limp "like a bastard." Though his mother "has ears like a goddam bloodhound," his parents are out and he enters Phoebe's room undetected.

Phoebe is asleep:

> She had her mouth way open. It's funny. You take adults, they look lousy when they're asleep and they have their mouths way open, but kids don't. Kids look all right. They can even have spit all over the pillow and they still look all right.

Suddenly Holden feels "swell" as he notices such things as Phoebe's discarded clothing arranged neatly on a chair. Throughout the Phoebe section, double entendres and sexually suggestive images and gestures multiply, most flowing naturally from Holden's mind while others, once the coding is perceived, become mechanical pointers to the psychological plot.

When Holden awakens Phoebe and is embarrassed by her overaffection, she eagerly tells him about the play in which she is "Benedict Arnold":

> "It starts out when I'm dying. This ghost comes in on Christmas Eve and asks me if I'm ashamed and everything. . . . Are you coming to it?"

When the Benedict Arnold image recurs at the end, we shall see that the role of "traitor" is precisely the one she must play if her brother is to weather his crisis. Phoebe then tells him about *The Doctor*, a movie she has seen "at the Lister Foundation" about

> "this doctor . . . that sticks a blanket over this child's face that's a cripple and can't walk. . . . and makes her suffocate. Then they make him go to jail for life imprisonment, but this child that he stuck the blanket over its head comes to visit him all the time and thanks him for what he did. He was a mercy killer."

This suggestive plot points to a horrible psychological possibility for Holden. He may "kill" Phoebe, pay his penalty agreeably, and even receive the gratitude of his victim. If interpretation here seems hard to justify, especially the implications of *Phoebe's* having suggested all this to Holden, consider the climax of the chapter in which Phoebe puts "the goddam pillow over her head" and refuses to come out. "She does that quite frequently," Holden reassures us—and then takes it all back: "She's a true madman sometimes." However innocent, Phoebe's responses to Holden's secret needs become the catalyst for both his breakdown and recovery.

Through the next chapter Phoebe hears Holden out on his "categorical aversions," in Salinger's phrase, to all the "phoniness" that has soured his world. The conversation begins in a curious manner:

> Then, just for the hell of it, I gave her a pinch on the behind. It was sticking way out in the breeze, the way she was

laying on her side. She has hardly any behind. I didn't do it hard, but she tried to hit my hand anyway, but she missed.

Then all of a sudden, she said, "Oh, why did you *do* it?" She meant why did I get the ax again. It made me sort of sad, the way she said it.

Holden spells out his dissatisfactions at length—and indeed he cites valid and depressing instances of human failings—until Phoebe challenges him several times, "You don't like *any*thing that's happening." "Name one thing," she demands. "One thing? One thing I like?" Holden replies. "Okay." At this point he finds he can't "concentrate too hot."

She was in a cockeyed position way the hell over the other side of the bed. She was about a thousand miles away.

He can't concentrate, I suggest, because the truth is too close.

About all I could think of were those two nuns that went around collecting dough in those beat-up old straw baskets. Especially the one with the glasses with those iron rims. And this boy I knew at Elkton Hills.

Repression has transferred the true thing he "likes a lot" to a nun, an inviolable "sister," who, we remember, had embarrassed Holden by talking about *Romeo and Juliet,* "that play [that] gets pretty sexy in parts." It may also be significant that *Romeo and Juliet* involves forbidden love that ends tragically— especially significant in connection with the other "thing" Holden thinks about, James Castle, the boy who had killed himself wearing Holden's turtleneck sweater.

None of this will do for Phoebe and she repeats the challenge:

"I like Allie," I said. "And I like doing what I'm doing right now. Sitting here with you, and talking, and thinking about stuff, and—"

When she objects that "Allie's dead," Holden tries to explain but gives up:

> "Anyway, I like it now," I said. "I mean right now. Sitting here with you and just chewing the fat and horsing—"

Her insistence drives him to the loveliest—and most sinister—fantasy in the novel:

> "You know that song 'If a body catch a body comin' through the rye'? I'd like—"

> "It's 'If a body *meet* a body coming through the rye!'" old Phoebe said.

Holden proceeds to conjure up the daydream of himself as catcher in the rye, the protector of childhood innocence. As Phoebe implies, however, the song is about romance, not romanticism. Because he has to, Holden has substituted a messianic motive for the true, erotic one.

In the next chapter Holden and Phoebe seem to be acting out a mock romance, much the way Seymour Glass does with the little girl in "A Perfect Day for Bananafish." The episode is at once movingly tender and ominous. Holden finds Phoebe "sitting smack in the middle of the bed, outside the covers, with her legs folded like one of those Yogi guys"—an image one critic interprets as making her an emblem of "the still, contemplative center of life." This may be valid for one level of Holden's mind. When he immediately asks her to dance, however, and "She practically jumped off the bed, and then waited while I took my shoes off," his excessive justifications point to guilt:

> I don't like people that dance with little kids. . . . Usually they keep yanking the kid's dress up in the back by mistake, and the kid can't dance worth a damn *any*way, and it looks terrible, but I don't do it out in public with Phoebe or anything. We just horse around in the house. It's different with

her anyway, because she can *dance*. She can follow anything you do. I mean if you hold her in close as hell so that it doesn't matter that your legs are so much longer. She stays right with you.

After the dance, Phoebe "jumped back in bed and got under the covers" and Holden "sat down next to her on the bed again . . . sort of out of breath." "'Feel my forehead,' she said all of a sudden." Phoebe claims she has learned to induce fever psychosomatically so that

"your whole forehead gets so hot you can burn somebody's hand."

That killed me. I pulled my hand away from her forehead, like I was in terrific danger. "Thanks for *tell*ing me," I said.

"Oh, I wouldn't've burned *your* hand. I'd've stopped before it got too—*Shhh!*" Then, quick as hell, she sat way the hell up in bed.

The parents have returned and the scene that follows, Holden gathering up his shoes and hiding in the closet as the mother interrogates Phoebe about the (cigarette) "smoke" in the bedroom and asks "were you warm enough?" is reminiscent of nothing so much as that mainstay of French farce, the lover hiding in the closet or under the bed as the girl ironically "explains" to husband or parent. More important are the implications of Phoebe's "heat." Though she cannot really induce it, her innocent compliance in the whole sexual charade does place Holden "in terrific danger."

When the mother leaves, Holden emerges from his hiding place and borrows money from Phoebe. Phoebe insists that he take all of her money and Holden "all of a sudden" begins to cry. . . .

Holden's breakdown, his visiting of his own suffering on the child, the chill air, and the innocence of their intimacy in this moving scene signal his growing, frightening awareness of the other sort of intimacy. From now until he sees Phoebe again, Holden is in full flight. Nonetheless, their parting is filled with suggestions of a sort one might expect after a casual, normal sexual encounter. (The emphases in the following passage are my own.)

> Then I *finished buttoning* my coat and all. I told her I'd *keep in touch with her.* She told me *I could sleep with her* if I wanted to, but I said no, that I'd better beat it. . . . Then I took my hunting hat out of my coat pocket and *gave it to her.* She likes those kind of crazy hats. She didn't want to take it, but *I made her.* I'll bet she *slept with it* on. She really likes those kinds of hats. Then I told her again I'd *give her a buzz* if I got a chance, and then I left.

It is almost as if Holden is acknowledging the real content of the sexual charade and escaping while he can. It would also seem that realization, however vague, is equated with deed as Holden immediately indicates that he wanted to be punished:

> It was a helluva lot easier getting out of the house than it was getting in, for some reason. For one thing, I didn't give much of a damn any more if they caught me. I really didn't. I figured if they caught me, they caught me. I almost wished they did, in a way.

Mr. Antolini's Advances Precipitate Holden's Breakdown

Holden leaves Phoebe to spend the night with Mr. Antolini, a former teacher who during the course of the evening offers sound if stilted assessments of Holden's future which become particularly relevant in the epilogue. Antolini has been drinking, however, and disrupts the peace he has provided (Holden feels sleepy for the first time) by awakening the boy with tentative homosexual advances. Certainly Holden is victimized ("I was shaking like a madman. . . . I think I was more depressed than I ever was in my life"), but the encounter may torment him most for its parallels to his own unconscious designs on a child. Now one begins to see the significance of Holden's unfounded suspicions about Jane Gallagher's stepfather and his murderous rage at the "perverty bum" who wrote the obscenity on Phoebe's school wall—inordinate reactions pointing to fears about himself.

At this point Holden's neurosis verges on madness. Each time he crosses a street, he imagines he will "disappear" and "never get to the other side of the street." I do not take this so much as a symbolic manifestation of "identity crisis" and of his fear that he "may never reach maturity"—although both are implicit—but rather as a literal, psychologically valid description of the boy's breakdown. He retreats into wild fantasies of running away forever, living in a cabin near, but not in, the woods ("I'd want it to be sunny as hell all the time"), and feigning deaf-muteness, all to escape the confusion about to engulf him. Phoebe betrays these plans—the first ironic level of the Benedict Arnold motif—by joining in his escape. When she appears, bag in hand and the hunting cap on her head, Holden reacts wildly:

"I'm going with you. Can I? Okay?"

"What?" I said. I almost fell over when she said that. I swear to God I did. I got sort of dizzy and I thought I was going to pass out or something again.

I thought I was going to pass out cold. I mean I didn't mean to tell her to shut up and all, but I thought I was going to pass out again.

I was almost all set to hit her. I thought I was going to smack her for a second. I really did. . . .

"I thought you were supposed to be Benedict Arnold in that play and all," I said. I said it very nasty. "Wuddaya want to do? Not be in the play, for God's sake?" That made her cry even harder. I was glad. All of a sudden I wanted her to cry till her eyes practically dropped out. I almost hated her. I think I hated her most because she wouldn't be in that play any more if she went away with me.

These near-hysterical responses can be understood, it seems to me, only in the context that Phoebe is the very thing he is fleeing. He somehow realizes that she *must* be his "Benedict Arnold."

Holden's fury at Phoebe having set the climax in motion, Salinger now employs a delicate spatial strategy. Phoebe returns the hat, turns her back on Holden, announces that she has no intention of running away with him, and runs "right the hell across the street, without even looking to see if any cars were coming." Positioning here signifies the end of their relation as possible lovers, but love remains. Holden does not go after her, knowing she'll follow him "on the *other* goddam side of the street. She wouldn't look over at me at all, but I could tell she was probably watching me out of the corner of her crazy eye to see where I was going and all. Anyway, we kept walking that way all the way to the zoo." They are still apart as they watch the sea lions being fed, Holden standing "right behind her." . . .

Holden promises not to run away and they rejoin as brother and sister in the presence of the carrousel—miraculously open in winter. Phoebe wants to ride and Holden finds a mature, new perspective:

> All the kids kept trying to grab for the gold ring, and so was old Phoebe, and I was sort of afraid she'd fall off the goddam horse, but I didn't say anything or do anything. The thing with kids is, if they want to grab for the gold ring, you have to let them do it, and not say anything. If they fall off, they fall off, but it's bad if you say anything to them.

The substitution of a gold ring for the traditional brass one may point to Phoebe's future as a woman. In any event, Holden has renounced his designs on Phoebe and thus abrogated his messianic role. Another Salinger story has young de Daumier-Smith relinquish his sexual designs on a nun with the announcement, "I am giving Sister Irma her freedom to follow her destiny. Everyone is a nun." One need not search for literary sources to recognize that the carrousel finally represents everyone's sacred, inviolable human destiny.

The Hunting Cap as Symbol of Holden's Human Resources

Readers now dubious about this paper's clinical approach ("aesthetic pathology," Salinger has called it) may wonder why I have thus far neglected to make a masculine symbol of Holden's long-peaked hunting cap—which he purchased, one recalls, after losing the fencing team's foils in a subway. This rather mechanical symbol does partake of the boy's masculinity or sexuality. But more than that, it becomes the most reliable symbolic designation of Holden's psychic condition through the novel. Ackley points out that it is a deer hunter's hat while Holden maintains that "This is a people shooting hat. . . . I shoot people in this hat." When one remembers that hunters wear red hats to keep from being shot and that Holden usually wears his backwards in the manner of a baseball catcher, the symbol embraces Holden's aggressive and withdrawing tendencies as well as the outlandish daydreams of becoming the messiah in the rye.

Holden's masculinity is plainly involved in such instances as when he has to retrieve the hat from under a bed after the fight with Stradlater and when it is entrusted to Phoebe's bed, but the symbol becomes more encompassing when she "restores" the hat in the climactic carrousel scene. . . .

At its deepest level, the hat symbolizes something like Holden's basic human resources—his birthright, that lucky caul of protective courage, humor, compassion, honesty, and love—all of which are the real subject matter of the novel.

As the symbolic hat gives Holden "quite a lot of protection, in a way" and he gets "soaked anyway," those human resources do not prevent emotional collapse. In the epilogue we learn that Holden went West—"after I went home, and . . . got sick and all"—not for the traditional opportunity there but for psychotherapy. This would be a bleak ending were it not for the fact that Holden has authored this structured narrative, just as Antolini predicted he might:

> "you'll find that you're not the first person who was ever confused and frightened and even sickened by human behavior. You're by no means alone on that score, you'll be excited and *stimulated* to know. Many, many men have been just as troubled morally and spiritually as you are right now. Happily, some of them kept records of their troubles. You'll learn from them—if you want to. Just as someday, if you have something to offer, someone will learn something from you. It's a beautiful reciprocal arrangement. And it isn't education. It's history. It's poetry."

The richness of spirit in this novel, especially of the vision, the compassion, and the humor of the narrator reveal a psyche far healthier than that of the boy who endured the events of the narrative. Through the telling of his story, Holden has given shape to, and thus achieved control of, his troubled past.

Holden Caulfield Is Unable to Cope with an Adult World

Peter J. Seng

Peter J. Seng taught at Connecticut College and is the author of numerous works of literary criticism, including Vocal Songs in the Plays of Shakespeare: A Critical History.

In this viewpoint Peter J. Seng contends that Holden Caulfield shares the same faults that he despises in others—phoniness and pretension. At the root of his mental breakdown, Seng asserts, is an inability to adjust to the realities of an adult world and to create satisfactory mature relationships. Seng believes that Holden will prevail, but that he must first acquire a sense of proportion in dealing with adult challenges and learn to love all of humanity with the love he has for children.

The plot of *The Catcher in the Rye* concerns the three-day odyssey of Holden Caulfield after he has been expelled from Pencey Prep for bad grades and general irresponsibility. At the beginning of the story Holden is in a sanitarium in California recovering from a mental breakdown. He says that he is not going to tell his life-story but just the story of "this madman stuff that happened to me around last Christmas just before I got pretty run-down and had to come out here and take it easy." In the final chapter he speculates about what he is going to do when he is released and reflects on "all this stuff I just finished telling you about. . . . If you want to know the truth, I don't *know* what I think about it." Between these important framing limits the story proper is contained. It reads like an edited psychoanalysis, an illusion which is sustained by the rambling first-person narrative.

Peter J. Seng, "The Fallen Idol: The Immature World of Holden Caulfield," *College English*, vol. 23, no. 3, December 1961, pp. 203–209.

Holden Caulfield Shares in the Phoniness He Despises

Sensitive and perceptive as Holden is, he is still an adolescent and so an immature judge of adult life. His viewpoint is as limited as that of [William] Hazlitt's young man who thinks that he will never die. Like many young people Holden is intolerant of sickness and the debility of old age. Recalling his visit to "Old Spencer" he says,

> there were pills and medicine all over the place, and every-thing smelled like Vicks Nose Drops. It was pretty depress-ing. I'm not too crazy about sick people, anyway. What made it even more depressing, old Spencer had on this very sad, ratty old bathrobe that he was probably born in or some-thing. I don't much like to see old guys in their pajamas and bath-robes anyway.

Nor can he bear the old history teacher's garrulity and physical habits. While Holden is quick to pass severe judgments on others he is not so quick to see the faults in himself. A number of the picayune traits he hates Ackley for in Chapter 3 are traits he reveals in himself in Chapter 4 when he talks to Stradlater. A comparison of these two chapters reveals interesting things both about Holden's character and about Salinger's narrative technique. It might be said that Holden's chief fault is his failure "to connect" (to use Forster's phrase); he hates lies, phoniness, pretense, yet these are often his own sins.

He is enraged at the thought that Stradlater may have "made time" with Jane Gallagher. His rage springs partly from the fact that he regards Jane as his own property, partly from his suspicion that Stradlater is a heel; yet there are further implications in this episode that he most deeply resents Stradlater's apparent self-possession in an area where he him-self is ill-at-ease. Stradlater may have "made time" with Jane (though the reader of the novel tends to see his testimony as an adolescent's boast); but the moment Holden arrives in New York he attempts to "make time" first with a burlesque stripper and then with a hotel call-girl. There is, to be sure, a difference in the objects of each boy's affections, but the difference is not so great as Holden, not "connecting," might think. His failure in both attempts is probably adequately explained by his confession:

> Sex is something I really don't understand too hot. You never know *where* the hell you are. I keep making up these sex rules for myself, and then I break them right away. Last year I made a rule that I was going to quit horsing around with girls that, deep down, gave me a pain in the ass. I broke it, though, the same week I made it. . . . Sex is something I just don't understand.

While Holden responds to the common chord to which all fleshly creatures vibrate, he is nonetheless contemptuous of its varied—and sometimes perverse—manifestations in others.

In a similar fashion he passes harsh verdicts on people who do not measure up to his standards of taste and urban sophistication. When the tourists from Seattle—Bernice, Marty, and Laverne (the very names spell out a whole aesthetic)—plan to see the first show at Radio City Music Hall their taste depresses him; yet the following day he goes there himself. Buying drinks for the girls from Seattle he puts on a pretense of New Yorkish world-weary sophistication. On the other hand he cannot bear that sort of pretense in others, and has only contempt for the kind of people who say that something is "grand," or affect a fashionable critical attitude about [Alfred] Lunt and [Lynn] Fontanne [husband and wife stage actors], or who make polite social noises at each other (social noises that have to be made if society is going to endure).

Holden Rejects the Adult World

What disturbs Holden about the world in which he finds himself is adults and adult values. He sees that the world belongs to adults, and it seems to him that they have filled it with phoniness, pretense, social compromise. He would prefer a world that is honest, sincere, simple. He is looking, as [critic Ihab H. Hassan] notes, for the "simple truth." Such a quest is doomed from the start: *there are no simple truths.* In a complex modern society truth, too, is complex, and a certain amount of social compromise is necessary.

This kind of civilizing compromise Holden is unwilling to make. The world he wants is a world of children or children-surrogates like the nuns. He would people it with little girls whose skates need tightening, little girls like his adored sister Phoebe; with little boys like the ones at the Museum of Natural History, filled with exquisite terror at the prospect of seeing the mummies. It would include small boys with poems on their baseball gloves like his brother Allie who died some years ago from leukemia and so has been arrested in permanent youth by death. The chief citizens of Holden's world would be the little boys who walk along the curbstone and sing,

If a body catch a body Coming through the rye.

Holden's chief fantasy is built on this memory: he sees himself as the "catcher in the rye," the only adult in a world of children:

I keep picturing all these little kids playing some game in this big field of rye and all. Thousands of little kids, and nobody's around—nobody big, I mean—except me. And I'm standing on the edge of some crazy cliff. What I have to do, I have to catch everybody if they start to go over the cliff—I mean if they're running and they don't look where they're going I have to come out from somewhere and *catch* them. That's all I'd do all day. I'd just be the catcher in the rye and all.

Holden has other fantasies as well, and these are less healthy. He imagines himself living all alone in a cabin in the far west pretending to be a deaf-mute. If anyone wanted to communicate with him, he says, that person would have to write him a note (a prescription that would also include his wife who would be deaf and dumb, too). "They'd get bored as hell doing that after a while, and then I'd be through with having conversations for the rest of my life." Both the "catcher" and the "deaf-mute" fantasies are rooted in a single desire: a wish to escape from an adult world with which Holden feels that he cannot cope.

Holden's Flaw Is His Inability to Accept Reality

His mental breakdown is a direct result of his inability to come to terms with adult reality. Consequently he invents other fantasies, tinged with paranoia, in which he sees himself as a martyr-victim. In front of Ackley he play-acts at going blind: "'Mother darling, give me your *hand*. Why won't you give me your hand?'" Roughed up by a pimp-bellhop he imagines that he has been shot, and fancies himself walking down the stairs of the hotel bleeding to death. In a third fantasy he imagines his own death and funeral in great detail. Finally, in his recollections of previous events he seems to identify with a schoolmate, James Castle, who jumped from a high window rather than submit to the brutality of prep school bullies.

The crucial chapter in *The Catcher in the Rye* seems to me to be the one in which Holden calls on his former English teacher Mr. Antolini. For all his own weaknesses Antolini sees to the heart of the matter and gives saving advice to Holden; the advice is rejected because Holden measures it against impossibly absolute standards. If this view of the novel is correct then Holden's interview with Antolini is also the high point of irony in *The Catcher in the Rye*: the proffered offer of salvation comes from a teacher whom Holden enormously admires, but the counsel is nullified when Holden discovers that Antolini, like all adults, has feet of clay. From the moment the boy leaves Antolini's apartment his mental breakdown commences. This sequence of events seems to be Salinger's intention.

If the Antolini episode is crucial, as I think it is, it deserves examination in some detail. The relationship between Mr. and Mrs. Antolini is immediately clear to the reader, if not to Holden. Mrs. Antolini is older than her husband and rich. They have an elegant apartment on Sutton Place, belong to the West Side Tennis Club in Forest Hills, and are ostentatiously affectionate in public. Yet in Holden's uncomprehending phrase, they are "never in the same room at the same time."

Holden's attachment to this teacher is in sharp contrast to his antipathy for "old Spencer" at the beginning of the novel. There is ease and *rapport* between the older man and the younger one. As Mrs. Antolini retires for the night to leave "the boys" alone, her husband has a stiff highball, obviously not his first. As he drinks he gives advice to Holden, all of it very much to the point:

> "I have a feeling that you're riding for some kind of a terrible, terrible fall. But I don't honestly know what kind. . . . It may be the kind where, at the age of thirty, you sit in some bar hating everybody who comes in looking as if he might have played football in college. Then again, you may pick up just enough education to hate people who say, 'It's a secret between he and I.' Or you may end up in some business office, throwing paper clips at the nearest stenographer."

It is instructive to re-examine the previous episodes of the novel in the light of this assessment of Holden's character. What Antolini predicts for the future already, in part, exists in the present. After another drink he goes on:

> "This fall I think you're riding for—it's a special kind of fall, a horrible kind. The man falling isn't permitted to feel or hear himself hit bottom. He just keeps falling and falling. The whole arrangement's designed for men who, at some time or other in their lives, were looking for something their

own environment couldn't supply them with. . . . So they gave up looking. They gave it up before they ever really even got started."

Antolini writes out for Holden an epigram from the works of the psychoanalyst Wilhelm Stekel: "'The mark of the immature man is that he wants to die nobly for a cause, while the mark of the mature man is that he wants to live humbly for one.'" This epigram is a penetrating insight into the personality of an adolescent who continually views himself as a martyr or savior, but never sees himself as modestly attempting to cope with a humdrum and very imperfect world. In effect what Antolini is saying is, "You are not alone; we have all been through this." You are not the first one, he tells Holden,

> "who was ever confused and frightened and even sickened by human behavior. You're by no means alone on that score, you'll be excited and *stimulated* to know. Many, many men have been just as troubled morally and spiritually as you are right now. Happily, some of them kept records of their troubles. You'll learn from them—if you want to."

He makes up a bed for the boy on the couch and then retires to the kitchen, presumably for another drink. Holden lies awake for a few seconds

> thinking about all that stuff Mr. Antolini'd told me. . . . He was really a pretty smart guy. But I couldn't keep my goddam eyes open, and I fell asleep.

That sleep is symbolic as well as literal. Suddenly waking during the night Holden finds Antolini sitting on the floor next to his couch-bed patting him on the head. Panicked by what he regards as something "perverty" he flees from the apartment.

The irony built into this denouement is clear: the saving advice that Antolini has given Holden has been rendered useless because the idol who gave it has fallen. Antolini is a shabby adult like all the others. In his reactions Holden is like the man in the Stephen Crane poem who climbed to the top of the mountain only to cry out:

> "Woe to my knowledge! I intended to see good white lands
> And bad black lands, But the scene is grey."

It is worth noting that Salinger takes pains to keep the end of the Antolini episode ambiguous: that is to say, while there can be little doubt in a reader's mind about Antolini's propensities, his gesture toward Holden is considerably short of explicit. In fact Salinger raises this very doubt in Holden's mind:

> I wondered if just maybe I was wrong about thinking he was making a flitty pass at me. I wondered if maybe he just liked to pat guys on the head when they're asleep. I mean how can you tell about that stuff for sure? You can't.

Whatever doubts he may have about Antolini's motives, there can be no doubts about the meaning of his own feelings as he walks up Fifth Avenue the next day:

> Then all of a sudden, something very spooky started happening. . . . Every time I came to the end of a block and stepped off the goddam curb, I had this feeling that I'd never get to the other side of the street. I thought I'd just go down, down, down, and nobody'd ever see me again.

This, of course, is the beginning of the fall which Antolini had predicted.

So much for the edited psychoanalysis of Holden Caulfield. It seems to me that if *The Catcher in the Rye* is viewed along the lines suggested above it is a moral novel in the fullest sense of that word. According to this interpretation Holden is not a mere victim of modern society, but is in some sense a tragic figure. His temporary mental defeat is brought about by a flaw in his own character: a naive refusal to come to terms with the world in which he lives. To regard him, on the other hand, as a pure young man who is martyred in his unavailing struggle against a sordid world of adult phoniness, is to strip him of any real dignity. Such an interpretation makes the novel guilty of idle romanticism. [Novelist and critic William Dean] Howells would have called it immoral romanticism because he would have seen it as filled with "idle lies about human nature and the social fabric," areas where we must know the truth if we are to deal "justly with ourselves and with one another."

Salinger himself is reported to have said that he regretted that his novel might be kept out of the reach of children. It is hard to guess at the motives behind his remark, but one of them may have been that he was trying to tell young people how difficult it was to move from their world into the world of adults. He may have been trying to warn them against the pitfalls of the transition. . . .

Holden will survive; but first he must learn to love other human beings as well as he loves children. He must acquire a sense of proportion, a sense of humor. He must learn compassion for the human, the pompous, the phoney, the perverse; such people are the fellow inhabitants of his world, and behind their pitiful masks are the faces of the children in the rye. In Stekel's phrase, he must learn to live humbly for a cause.

Holden Caulfield Is Afraid of Growing Up and Competing in an Adult World

Joanne Irving

Joanne Irving is a psychologist and cofounder of the Chrysalis Group, a coaching and consulting firm.

Joanne Irving offers an interpretation of The Catcher in the Rye *based on the psychoanalytical theories of Alfred Adler. Adler was an Austrian psychologist who introduced the term "inferiority feeling" and developed a psychotherapy designed to direct those suffering from feelings of inferiority back to emotional health. Irving contends that Holden Caulfield has strong feelings of inferiority, which she traces to dynamics present in his family situation. Along with these feelings of inferiority, Irving suggests, Holden has extremely high goals of superiority, most notably stated by his desire to be the "catcher in the rye." Adolescence, according to Adler, is a time when socially balanced people confront the life tasks of sex/love and occupation. Holden does not want to grow up and take on these life tasks, Irving argues, and this is the source of his depression.*

This paper will be an [Alfred] Adlerian interpretation of Holden Caulfield, the 17-year-old tragic hero of *The Catcher in the Rye* by J.D. Salinger. We will examine how Holden's mistaken life style results in his resorting to neurosis in order to deal with the particular life problems he faces. Holden's extremely high goal of superiority, his excessive feelings of inferiority, and his diminished social interest lead him to attempt to solve problems on the useless side of life. We

Joanne Irving, "*The Catcher in the Rye*: An Adlerian Interpretation," *Journal of Individual Psychology*, vol. 32, May 1976, pp. 81–92. Copyright © 1976 by the University of Texas Press. All rights reserved. Reproduced by permission of the University of Texas Press.

will also consider some of the factors which contributed to Holden's original mistaken attitudes, such as his family constellation and childhood pampering. . . .

Family Constellation

An individual's style of life is formed at an early age and remains his way of dealing with the world. Holden is the second born of four children. While birth order is not destiny, it is important to realize that a child's psychological place in the family influences the attitudes he has and thus his life style. The family is the child's first social environment.

We do not know anything about Holden's relationship with his older brother when they were young, but Holden now seems to respect and admire D.B. He quotes him as an authority on good restaurants and good books and says "My favorite author is my brother." But Holden also resents his brother because he has a successful career writing movies. "He's out in Hollywood being a prostitute. If there's one thing I hate, it's the movies." Holden may be disappointed that his brother chose a commercial career, or perhaps Holden is really envious of this older brother who has "lots of dough" and drives a sporty car. Holden repeats so often that he hates the movies that we suspect it's an accusation against others for liking them.

As the younger brother of D.B., Holden is in quite a race. His pace-setter for achievement has achieved much success in society. Holden's striving for superiority is going to be under pressure, as he competes with his older brother. The result of this competition depends on Holden's courage and self confidence. We can see that Holden feels discouraged when he says such things as, "As a matter of fact, I'm the only dumb one in the family." "Dumb" seems to include more than simply lack of intelligence; it seems to indicate that he is the worst at everything.

In *Problems of Neurosis,* Adler notes, "If the second child loses hope of equality, he will . . . tend to escape to the useless side of life, and . . . laziness or lying will pave the way to neurosis and self destruction." Holden tells us:

> I'm the most terrific liar you ever saw in your life. . . . If I'm on my way to the store to buy a magazine, even, and somebody asks me where I'm going, I'm liable to say I'm going to the opera.

He lies to the woman he meets on the train just so he can have something to talk about, and he lies when he's in a situation that he can't handle by saying that he's just had a serious operation. This clearly is a way Holden strives for superiority on the useless side of life. He brags that he is the best liar. Lying seems to be a way that Holden can feel superior because he controls the situation. Only he knows the truth so he can dominate and manipulate others. He can save face, cover any feelings of inferiority by lying. . . .

Holden is not only a second born child however, he is also a middle child. Allie and Phoebe were both younger than him. Allie died of leukemia four years ago when he was eleven and Holden was thirteen. Phoebe is only ten, seven years younger than Holden. The distance between them now would suggest that he is not in competition with them. Holden describes them both as "sweet," and "intelligent" and says that "everyone" agrees.

When Holden is feeling what he describes as "lonesome and depressed" and what we would say is particularly inferior, he thinks of Allie and Phoebe. He has two early recollections of Allie that support the idea that Holden's younger siblings are "sweet" because they admire and like him, that is, they make him feel superior. The first recollection is a very short scene of Allie sitting on a fence watching Holden tee off his golf game. Holden says he knew that Allie would be there when he looked behind him. The little brother is looking up to the big brother in admiration of his abilities, while big brother looks back at him. In the second scene, Holden remembers the time when he wouldn't let Allie come with him on a fishing trip. He told Allie that he was just a child, too little to ride that far on his bike. When Holden is depressed he starts talking to Allie and says, "Okay. Go home and get your bike and meet me in front of Bobby's house." Holden remembers when Allie wanted to be like him, to do things with him, and looked up to him. Holden feels superior in both scenes. He tells Allie to get his bike now because he misses the appreciator he had in Allie. When Allie died, Holden spent the night in the garage and broke all the windows with his bare hands. This is a rather exaggerated response to even the loss of a much cared for brother. It can be assumed that in addition to losing a beloved brother, Holden also lost a source of superior feelings when Allie died.

Holden's relationship with Phoebe appears to be similar to that which he had with Allie. Phoebe too admires and emulates him. She skates where he skated and "If you tell Phoebe something, she knows exactly what the hell you're talking about." In other words, Phoebe agrees with him.

In contrast to adults whom he almost always calls "phonies," Holden says, "God, I love it when a kid's nice and polite when you tighten their skate for them or something. Most kids are. They really are." Holden's feelings of inferiority are so great that he only feels fond of Phoebe and Allie because they are younger than him. He feels affectionate because he can be superior to them, benevolent, but nonetheless, superior. According to Adler, "Children who have a great feeling of inferiority want to exclude stronger children and play with weaker children." Holden is 17 years old, but he seems to be just such a child.

Pampering Mother

Though we know little about Holden's mother, he offers some information that indicates indirectly that he was a pampered child. For example, his mother was apparently overattentive to his needs as he says, "... my mother, all you have to do to my mother is cough somewhere in Siberia and she'll hear you. She's nervous as hell." He also tells us that mothers only see good in their sons and describes his mother and grandmother buying him presents and giving him lots of money. When Phoebe disobeys Mrs. Caulfield, she simply says "I don't like it" and changes the subject. Pampering leads to a self-centeredness and impaired social interest and leaves the child feeling uncertain because he is excused from responsibility. The child feels special, that he deserves the best and thus sets his goal of superiority accordingly high. Holden tells us:

> I still act sometimes like I was only twelve. Everybody says that.... Sometimes I act a lot older than I am—I really do—for people never notice it. People never notice anything.

These are the words of the pampered child who wants to be praised for all his accomplishments and who is angry and accusatory when he feels he is not getting adequate recognition.

The Adlerian perspective emphasizes the "key role the mother must play in preparing her child for a life of cooperation and contribution." By her example, Mrs. Caulfield teaches Holden how to deal with life crises. Holden describes how at first his "mother gets very hysterical," and in general "she's very nervous." In this first relationship where he should be learning cooperation and trust, Holden learns that one can use nervousness, the weapon of weakness, in difficult situations. Holden applies this lesson using depression as his way of coping.

Holden used his own creative abilities to interpret his mother's attentions as pampering. He has selected from her behavior the lesson that being nervous or hysterical is a way of dealing with problems. Thus, when faced with a situation that he feels inadequately prepared for, Holden lacks cooperation and uses symptomatology.

Inferiority-Superiority Dynamics

Holden's oversized inferiority feelings are in contrast to his extremely high goals of superiority. Thus he is sure to feel small and inferior. Adler comments that an inferiority complex "burdens the character with oversensitivity, leads to egotistical self considerations and self-reflections, (and) lays the foundation for neurosis." We can certainly see that Holden does have this foundation. His oversensitivity to the social amenities which he considers hypocritical leads him to say, "I can't stand that stuff. It drives me crazy." He has a similar reaction to people saying "Good luck" or "grand" to him. That he is overly involved in self consideration is illustrated time and time again as he describes his acute awareness of what he looks like, what he does in any situation. His marked inferiority complex is obvious when he comments that if life is a game then he's on the wrong side. This surely is what Adler refers to when he says that the person with great inferiority feelings "lives, as it were, in an enemy country." Holden's strong temper and passion, illustrated by the fist fight he gets into with his roommate because he dates a friend of Holden's; and his constant motion, wandering through New York City and from school to school, also indicate his deep sense of inferiority.

In contrast to these profound feelings of inferiority are Holden's extremely high goals of superiority. This goal shows itself frequently during his story. . . .

Perhaps the best example of how lofty Holden's goals are is the scene he describes to Phoebe when she challenges him to name one thing he'd like to be. He replies:

> Anyway, I keep picturing all these little kids playing some game in this big field of rye and all. Thousands of little kids, and nobody's around—nobody big, I mean—except me. And I'm standing on the edge of some crazy cliff. . . . I have to catch everybody if they start to go over the cliff—I mean if they're running and they don't look, where they're going. . . .

Consistent with Holden's expression of love for his younger brother and sister and children in general, is his desire to be the only big person around. Holden's goal of superiority, to be the big hero and to have everyone's destiny in his control is obvious. Clearly it is removed from possibility, removed from common sense, and hence, he can only attempt to realize it on the useless side of life.

Lack of Social Interest

Holden's lack of social interest, that is, lack of feeling of fellowship and empathy with others, has been implied in most of his story. It is further illustrated by the fact that all of his contacts with people are disappointing. For example, he says, "Almost everytime somebody gives me a present, it ends up making me sad." He feels lonely: "I felt so lonesome, all of a sudden. I almost wished I was dead." These experiences are the result of his rejection of society. ". . . if I were a piano player . . . and all these dopes thought I was terrific, I'd hate it." At no time does Holden express any concern for anybody but himself. Only once does he do anything nice for another person. That was when he bought a record for Phoebe, but he breaks it by accident before he gets it home. Typical of the neurotic, Holden expresses his lack of social interest in overgeneralizations about the way people are. Throughout his story, Holden says such things as:

people always ruin things

people never think anything is anything *really*

people are always hot to have a discussion when you're not

people never believe you

Clearly, Holden lacks the courage to cooperate in an adult world.

We have referred to a difficult situation that has precipitated Holden's developing symptoms. In this case, the exogenous factors do not seem to be so much related to a particular incident as they do to Holden's age. His first symptoms appeared at age thirteen, the onset of puberty and when he was first sent to prep school. Two of the three major life tasks come into focus at this time in life and Holden seems ill prepared to meet them.

The task of occupation is presented because Holden is enrolled in a school which is designed to help him prepare for college and hence, an occupation. He must stop being a little boy and begin making specific plans about what he wants for an occupation. He must succeed in prep school in order to live up to the expectations of an upper-middle class male. Holden has been expelled from four such schools. The experiences he describes occur just after he has flunked out of the fourth school and must go home and face his parents. We know that he excels in English and that he places a high value on being intelligent, but his fear of not being superior causes him to act lazy so he will have an excuse if he fails. Holden describes all the schools as being full of "phonies," criticizes their procedures, and generally expresses anger towards everything they represent. He participates in only the less admirable adult behavior such as smoking, swearing, and drinking. In this way he can justify not accepting the responsibility that prep school requires. He strives to be superior on the useless side of life.

The other task that Holden must actively deal with is sex and love. Not only has he reached the age of sexual maturity, but he is also in a situation where he has the opportunity to get involved in intimate relationships with the opposite sex. Sex, women, and love are the most common topics of conversation at this all-male school. Holden's peers all express their opinions about this issue and thus he is challenged to make some decisions about how he will approach this problem of life. In this task, too, Holden must give up being a little boy and assume some adult responsibility. . . .

Antithetical Thinking

Adler has noted that neurotic patients only know contradiction and antithesis [opposition]. Because Holden finds maturing and facing adult responsibilities too difficult, he describes all of adulthood as phony while being childlike is genuine. We see that Holden does not want to grow up when he describes why he likes the museum: because "everything always stayed right where it was." The carrousel, too, is nice because it always plays the same song, "Certain things they should stay just as they are," he says.

Holden's great feelings of inferiority and his high goals of superiority combined with his lack of social interest result in his inability to deal with the life tasks of sex and occupation in a useful way. He hesitates to grow up; however he must develop excuses in order to save face. He must reject adulthood by defining it as less desirable than childhood. . . .

Senseless Plans

Holden now makes two rather senseless plans to run away from having to live a cooperative life in society. In them we see how desperate he is feeling, how far from common sense he has moved, and how really neurotic he is. His first plan is to run away to Vermont, where he thinks he can avoid people. He fails to think about how he would support himself and abandons the idea when Sally refuses to accompany him. His second plan is to hitch hike out West and get a job. "I didn't care what kind of job it was, though. Just so people didn't know me and I didn't know anybody. . . . I'd pretend I was one of those deaf-mutes," so he wouldn't have to talk to anyone. He goes on to say that he would have a rule that "nobody could do anything phony" when they visited him. "If anybody tried to do anything phony, they couldn't stay." All the time he is making this plan, he is walking through the streets of New York talking to his dead brother, saying, "Allie, please don't let me disappear." Holden's useless goal of superiority becomes clear. He is so ill prepared to face life's tasks that he feels he needs to control everyone around him. If he feels that they place any demands on him he will label them as phony and isolate himself from them. This is the only way he can continue to appear superior with such extraordinary feelings of inferiority. He fears that otherwise he will disappear.

Holden's story ends when the one person with whom he still feels good, the one person who makes him appear superior, challenges him. Phoebe shows him that he has rejected everything and yet she refuses to let him find excuses or run away. He cannot label her phony because she admires him too much. He cannot escape from his responsibilities because she insists on following him when he tries to run away. He has no choice but to relinquish his excuses and go home. "I felt so damn happy all of a sudden. . . . I was damn near bawling, I felt so damn happy, if you want to know the truth. I don't know why," the certain relief of having been discovered.

Holden completes the novel by saying that he went home, got sick, and came to "this Place." The exact nature of those symptoms we don't know, but they seem unimportant because we can be sure that they support the pattern we have seen.

Holden Feels Inferior and Profoundly Discouraged

An Adlerian interpretation has been made of the life of Holden Caulfield as he presents it in *Catcher in the Rye*. As the second son in the family, Holden has lost confidence in himself. He feels discouraged and thus adopts a life style based on a mistaken way of feeling superior. He resorts to lies and rebellion. He is able to feel fond of his younger brother and sister because they admire him and hence make him appear superior.

The pampering Holden received and/or interpreted in his childhood contributed to his self centeredness and impaired social interest. Holden wants to continue being the pampered baby and so is faced with quite a predicament when he is expected to assume some adult responsibilities at prep school. His experiences in childhood have helped prepare him to deal with such a quandary since he has a mother who handles problems by being nervous.

Holden demonstrates his feelings of extreme inferiority in a number of ways. His oversensitivity implies an accusation against others for being phony and driving him crazy. He has a strong temper and thus gets into arguments and fights wherever he goes. In short, Holden acts as if he were living in an enemy country where anyone could attack him. "Attack" in this sense means expose his inferiority.

Holden's lofty goals of superiority are illustrated by his fantasies. He imagines himself the tragic hero with a bullet in his guts and as the catcher in the rye. Holden presents himself as the only genuine and sensitive person in a world of phonies. By hating society, Holden is able to pretend that he is superior without having to be competent. He shines more rather than being more because he lacks adequate social interest to deal with adult problems in a productive way.

When Holden reaches adolescence and must face the life tasks of sex and occupation, he is unprepared. At this age, Holden must give up his childish ways and accept some adult independence. He is faced with the decision of how he is going to relate with the opposite sex and how he is going to prepare himself for a career. But Holden does not want to grow up. He is too self centered, and too invested in appearing superior to risk competing in the adult world.

Confronted with this situation, Holden must create excuses in order to avoid these tasks. His feelings of inferiority are so great that he is afraid he will not succeed. Without social interest, Holden lacks the courage to grow up. Thus, Holden becomes a bitter, hateful young man. He defines the adult world as disgusting, boring, and most of all, phony. He runs away from school, from his family, from his friends, and finally, himself. This brings on the onset of his neurotic symptoms which he simply describes as being "sick." The Adlerian perspective shows that Holden does not get sick, but rather he suffers from profound discouragement about growing up.

Holden Caulfield Is Dealing with the Expected Psychological Angst of Adolescence

Peter Shaw

Peter Shaw was Will and Ariel Durant Professor of Humanities at St. Peter's College. He is the author of The Character of John Adams *and* The War Against the Intellect: Episodes in the Decline of Discourse.

Peter Shaw believes that many critics have been overly clinical in their assessments of Holden Caulfield, failing to take into account that adolescence is a time of dramatic mood swings approaching schizophrenia. Holden's behavior, in fact, can be explained because he is dealing with two important psychological experiences of adolescence—mourning the loss of his childhood and being in love. Shaw states that at times Holden is a reliable social critic, and at other times he is unreliable. He finds that Holden tends to be most reliable when dealing with the world of children, and less reliable when addressing the adult world.

Holden's psychologically disturbed state has been advanced [by critics] as the source both of his insight and of his lack of insight. The lines have been sharply drawn between Holden as an insightful social critic and as a mistaken projector of his own frailties onto society. Since evidence can be found to support each of these analyses, it might follow that Holden is an inconsistently drawn character. Yet he has never struck readers this way. How, then, can the opposite impressions of consistency and inconsistency in his character be reconciled?

Peter Shaw, *New Essays on The Catcher in the Rye*. New York: Cambridge University Press, 1991. Copyright © 1991 Cambridge University Press. Reprinted with the permission of Cambridge University Press.

Teenage Years Are a Complex Time

The answer to this question, I wish to argue, lies in the peculiar dynamics of adolescent psychology. The teenage years stand out as life's most complicated and tortured period. It has been said that teenage behavior, with its swings into and out of rationality, actually resembles schizophrenia. Certainly, this is the one period of life in which abnormal behavior is common rather than exceptional. It is no wonder, then, that young readers and professional critics alike have been able to regard Holden as normal despite his own conviction that he is not—or that other readers have been able to regard him primarily as a disturbed youth even though he often talks sense.

Failing to take into account the normality of abnormality in adolescence, the psychoanalytic critics in particular have taken a too purely clinical approach to Holden. E.H. Miller's positing of a life crisis dominated by mourning and guilt over the death of Allie, for example, seems too comprehensive and too definitive. For although Allie's death might be cited to account for much of Holden's behavior, no single act or expression of his stands out as inexplicable without reference to Allie. His brother's death exacerbates rather than constitutes Holden's adolescent crisis.

The psychoanalytic essays rest narrowly on single explanations, and disagree with one another. Nevertheless, their notation of classical symptoms in Holden should make it impossible for critics any longer to ignore the importance of psychological processes in both Holden's behavior and his ideas. Miller, for example, is able to call attention to at least fifty mentions by Holden of being depressed, repeated references on his part to himself and others as "crazy," and "his repeated use of variations on the phrase 'that killed me.'" One can add that Holden's disturbed condition is also evoked by a pattern of verbal slips, double entendres, errors, forgettings, accidents, and fallings down. The most striking of his double entendres, redolent both of guilt over Allie's death and an attempt to fob off that guilt on someone else, is a remark about his sister Phoebe containing the words, "she killed Allie, too." Of course he means by "killed" that she amused Allie. But his unconscious understanding is that Phoebe (like himself) is somehow responsible for Allie's death. . . .

Mourning and Being in Love Are Stages in Maturation

As with the rest of his behavior, Holden's self-punishments have some reference to guilt over Allie's death, as well as having a source in adolescent psychology. "The adolescent," writes Peter Blos in *On Adolescence: A Psychoanalytic Interpretation*, "incurs a real loss in the renunciation of his oedipal parents, and he experiences the inner emptiness, grief, and sadness which is part of all mourning." The adolescent also mourns for his own earlier childhood. If *The Catcher in the Rye* is, as E. H. Miller argues, about Holden's need "to bury Allie before he can make the transition to adulthood," it is also about Holden's need to bury and mourn other elements of his past. The elements link up with memories of Allie, pushing Holden toward breakdown yet always rendering his experience recognizable.

But mourning is only one of the two main psychological experiences typical of Holden's stage of adolescence. The other is "being in love." If Holden is unable to move on from mourning, he is equally unable to commence the being-in-love portion of his maturation process. He is suffering through what [renowned psychologist] Erik Erikson calls "the prime danger of this age": an excessively prolonged "moratorium" [period during which an activity is halted] on growing up. (Such prolongation can also be referred to as a "moratorium of illness.")

Holden expresses his need for moratoriums on both death and love in his two museum visits. The first visit is to the Museum of Natural History, whose dioramas of American Indian life convey an image of time suspended. The Indian who is fishing and the squaw who is weaving will never change, he muses, and he goes on to fantasize returning to the dioramas, without growing older, and finding the figures always exactly the same. Their perfection stands against the disturbing implications of a different couple—Holden's parents. He imagines himself making one of his trips to view the museum figures after hearing his "mother and father having a terrific fight in the bathroom." The mature life of couples, in other words, presents a threatening prospect relieved by contemplating the Indian mother and father in the museum. Their serene sameness evokes an imagined, permanent moratorium on love and its consequences.

At the Metropolitan Museum of Art, Holden leads two little boys to the reconstructed pharaonic tomb and its collection of mummies. When the boys run away in fright at his account of mummification (characteristically the only information about Ancient Egypt he could recall for his history examination), he finds that he "liked it" in the tomb: "it was so nice and peaceful." Here is a place in which he can finally rest in untroubled communion with eternal death: he is alongside mummies preserved as he wishes Allie could be preserved, and symbolizing his own wish to be preserved from change. Very soon, though, like his other moments of suspension, this one is rudely interrupted. He is driven from the tomb when a scrawled "F--- you" graffito catches his eye. Not for the first time the insistent reminder of sex drives him reluctantly back into life—this time to the bathroom where he faints in a purgative ritual that marks his first emergence from his moratorium.

Holden's clinging to the part of his moratorium that concerns sex is expressed in his curious fondness for his friend Jane Gallagher's keeping her kings in the back row when playing checkers. Jane is the girl he has kissed on only one occasion, but whose date with his roommate makes him frantic, and whom he cannot quite bring himself to phone after he runs away from school. . . .

Jane's withholding her kings may be said to symbolize the suspension of maturation typical of this adolescent period— even as it typifies the static, sexually unthreatening relationship Holden has had with her. For, like young people, the pieces on a checkerboard must keep moving forward. Or, as the game's technical term has it, they must keep "developing." On reaching the back row they have in effect achieved maturity, and are accordingly "kinged." By not moving her kings out of the back row, Jane solves the problem presented by this unavoidable process of maturation. She has made it one of *arrested development*. Understandably, this is particularly attractive to Holden.

Holden's catcher in the rye fantasy is usually understood to contain a kind of moratorium idea. The children falling off the cliff are said to symbolize a fall into adulthood, from which Holden imagines himself sparing them even as he would spare himself. But it is possible to be more specific: in psychological terms the "catcher" passage combines the elements both of falling in love and of mourning. To see how this is so, it is important to notice the source of the fantasy— Holden's watching a couple and their child—in order to track the unconscious allusive trail leading to love and death. Holden recalls walking along Fifth Avenue one day and observing with pleasure and empathy a couple and their playful child. To begin with, the family is not well off, Holden observes. This connects its members to the series of underdogs Holden has been attracted to, starting with fellow students at Pencey Prep, and extending to characters in movies and books. Furthermore, the child, at the moment he is observed, is a kind of outcast in the family itself—"walking alone" while the parents "were just walking along, talking, not paying any attention to their kid."

The child is also in danger. . . .

Guilt of the Survivor

Viewing the catcher fantasy psychologically, E. H. Miller puts it that "Holden has the 'crazy' idea that he should have saved Allie." But psychoanalytically speaking, the process leading to the fantasy of rescue would have to be described as somewhat more complicated. The child whose sibling dies commonly suffers not so much the guilt of having failed to effect a rescue as that of having at some time harbored the wish that the sibling might die. (When Allie died, Holden's immediate reaction had been to punish himself by slamming his fist through the garage windows, prompting his parents to think of having him psychoanalyzed.) The actual death, no matter what its cause (Allie had died of leukemia), can lead to a reaction formation, that is, to the creation of an opposite wish. The wish to kill, for example, can be replaced by a wish to rescue. Allie is the source of the rescue fantasy, then, but not its object.

In Holden's case the reaction formation manifested in the catcher fantasy is combined with another kind of guilt that may follow the death of a sibling, that felt by virtue of being a survivor. Such guilt often leads to an avoidance of success—as when Holden repeatedly fails out of schools—or else to imagining oneself incapable of success at an ordinary vocation. Being a catcher in the rye, no ordinary vocation, provides a bridge from guilty failure to success of a psychologically acceptable kind.

The being-in-love aspect of the catcher passage emerges from the prominent but neglected circumstance of its connection with the series of errors and slips revealing of Holden's unconscious. As Phoebe points out to him just before he recounts the fantasy, he has misheard the little boy sing "if a body *catch* a body":

"It's 'If a body *meet* a body coming through the rye'!" old Phoebe said. "It's a poem. By Robert *Burns*."

Holden answers: "I *know* it's a poem by Robert Burns." He knows the words, as would anyone his age at the time *The Catcher in the Rye* takes place. The song and its words were a standard tune of the day—of the sort sung around the piano at home. One understands that its words would come easily, and correctly, to the lips even of the little boy whom Holden mishears.

What, then, is the significance of Holden's error? The phrase "meet a body" conjures up not only a meeting between a lad and a lass, but because of the suggestiveness of "body" when detached from its Scottish meaning of "person," the phrase implies the coming together of male and female bodies. The next line of the song—"If a body kiss a body, need a body cry"—makes explicit the romantic/sexual context of the first. This is why Holden catches only the one line, and that one imperfectly. Unconsciously suppressing the word "meet," he avoids the very matter of his relations with girls, which he has been unable to resolve. "Meet" acts as another reminder, like the "F--- you" graffiti that keep confronting him, of the disturbing sexual basis of love. Each time, Holden experiences a need to "erase" the reminder. And each time his need has reference to young people. The first graffito, after all, appears on a wall at his sister's school, and it is to protect youngsters that he is moved to erase it. His fantasy of rescue in the rye comes out of the same impulse to protect youngsters (and the youngster in himself) from vulgarized sexual knowledge.

Earlier, Holden has confronted the vulgarized kind of knowledge in his roommate Stradlater, who seems to have kissed a body: Jane Gallagher. To the question "if a body kiss a body need a body cry?" the answer, one may say, is "yes." For when Holden imagines not just a kiss but Stradlater and Jane having sex, he does end up "practically bawling" (after maneuvering Stradlater into beating him up). Once again he himself,

Jared Leto during the filming of the movie "Chapter 27," which is a movie about Mark David Chapman in the days leading up to the murder of John Lennon. The film is partly inspired by Chapman's reading of the novel, The Catcher in the Rye, *which deals with psychological angst and severe depression.* Getty Images.

having had a relationship with Jane that only once reached the stage of (chaste) kissing, is frozen at a painful stage of development. In contrast, Stradlater has, to Holden's dismay, broken through this stage. Accordingly, when Stradlater hints at having had sex with Jane, Holden takes a swing at him: "I told him he didn't even care if a girl kept all her kings in the back row or not."

Holden has idealized Jane in a typical adolescent way, for "to adolescence proper belongs that unique experience, tender love," writes Peter Blos. But the adolescent boy must progress from an early "state of infatuation toward the fusion of tender and sexual love." Having participated in Stradlater's splitting off of tender love from his sexual intentions toward Jane, Holden has maneuvered Stradlater into hitting him in order to be punished for this violation of Jane. The fusion of tender and sexual love remains difficult for Holden. It represents a vertiginous, dangerous kind of falling for him: the extreme of the suggestion contained in the words "falling in love."

The Theme of Falling

The theme of falling extends from the catcher fantasy, to being knocked down by Stradlater, to the threat of falling off the curb while walking up Fifth Avenue (with the related threat of falling out of sanity and consciousness), to a series of trippings and pratfalls suffered by Holden in the course of his adventures. These falls convey adolescent sexual awkwardness—almost explicitly so when Holden trips over his suitcase on the way to letting a prostitute into his hotel room. . . .

Holden not only falls inadvertently in minor ways; he is repeatedly drawn toward catastrophic forms of falling. Each time, he is searching out self-punishment for his unconscious guilt over Allie's death. The wish to be punished by death accounts for his apparently illogical response to Phoebe's accusation that he doesn't like "*any*thing that's happening." "I do!" he insists. But she challenges him to "name one thing." He has trouble "concentrating" on an answer, but then James Castle pops into his mind: this is a fellow student who leaped to his death. Clearly, Holden is half in love with easeful death.

At the same time, of course, he half hopes to be saved. On sneaking out of his parents' apartment after talking to Phoebe, he admits that "for some reason," at this point "I didn't give a damn any more if they caught me." Then, fixing on the word he has uttered, he adds: "I figured if they caught me, they caught me. I almost wished they did, in a way." As much as he needs to fall, in other words, Holden needs to be caught. (Horsing around at school, he has expressed the same need. Pulling his cap down over his eyes, "I started groping around in front of me, like a blind guy. . . . I kept saying, 'Mother darling, why won't you give me your *hand*?'")

Besides rescuing children from maturation, Holden may be said to be rescuing others in one further sense deriving from young love. "The sensitive adolescent who cannot yet fall in love with a specific person on a realistic basis," writes Theodore Lidz,

> . . . can experience a more diffuse love of nature or of mankind in which there is a vague seeking for expression and fulfillment of the feelings that are surging within him. He feels that he must lose himself in nature or find ways of giving himself in the service of mankind.

The Adolescent Messiah

The desire to serve mankind can lead to messianism, perhaps in the form of joining a cult or fringe political organization, or else it can eventuate in fantasies of service. In its negative form the same displacement of love leads to delinquency or running away from school. Holden moves in each of the negative directions, both running away and fantasizing himself a rescuer.

The phenomenon of adolescent messianism stands out as the single analytical conception actually referred to in *The Catcher in the Rye*. It is, in fact, the centerpiece of the one, serious, considered evaluation of Holden by another character—his former teacher, Antolini. In the course of an analysis of Holden that includes an emphasis on the imminence of his suffering some kind of "fall" (a usage that alerts the reader to a wide-ranging play on the meanings of this word), Antolini writes out for him some words "written by a psychoanalyst named Wilhelm Stekel": "The mark of the immature man is that he wants to die nobly for a cause, while the mark of the mature man is that he wants to live humbly for one." The words capture the perfectionist urge in Holden, yet misrepresent him as leaning toward a messianism of action when actually his tendency is toward fantasies of rescue quite divorced from any social idea or cause.

The same distinction between action and fantasy applies to Holden's critique of society, which is sometimes taken to represent a reformist impulse, a wish for a better world. A careful scrutiny of Holden's dislikes, complaints, observations, and especially his generalizations about the world, however, reveals many of them to be personal. This is another way of saying that Holden is a first-person narrator of a particular kind. In novels with first-person narrators the common disparity is between the narrator's reports of what he observes (which are dependable) and his opinions (which are undependable). With Holden, there is additionally a range of reliability among his opinions depending on who and what he is evaluating. . . .

Holden as a Critic of Society

Holden is insightful, it seems, where children are concerned, but less so with adults, especially parents (except when they are with their children). Similarly, he feels sympathy for the outcasts of life and literature—Hamlet, for example—but lacks sympathy for anyone who does not display a psychological disturbance—Romeo, for example. . . .

An examination of Holden's critique of society, then, shows him to be by turns merely irritable and positively insightful. Just as with the question of his sanity, there is evidence both for those who find him an admirable social critic and for those who do not. And once again the variability in question turns out to involve adolescent psychology—if not exclusively the realm of the adolescent moratorium. Taken as a whole, Holden's critique can be seen to relate to the sexually repressive component of his extended moratorium. His repression is manifested not only in his chaste relationship with Jane but also in his wish to become a monk, his preference for the two (nonsexual) nuns he meets over the other women, and his dismissal of the prostitute sent to his hotel room. As it happens, adolescent repression of sexuality, especially when tinged with an attraction to the ascetic, often produces exactly what Holden is known for: a tendency to deliver "negative judgments" on the world.

If it has to be said that Holden's vision is often linked to personal and psychological sources, the feeling of most readers that he is somehow right about things in general cannot altogether be dismissed. Salinger himself has conveyed an impression of Holden's being right, possibly because he shifted in the course of writing from a noncommittal authorial distance to a perilously close identification with his protagonist. . . .

The Catcher in the Rye presents society and its figures of authority as both right and wrong. They are right that Holden's extended adolescent moratorium must come to an end, but surely wrong to dismiss him as a merely confused adolescent. For he is undergoing a special combination of kinds of mourning—for his brother Allie, for his own earlier childhood self, and for his parents as the revered figures of his youth—and his mourning has acted on his sensibility in strikingly creative ways. Such creativity, too, is a normal—if rare— accompaniment of adolescence.

As for Holden himself, he too is both right and wrong. He sometimes has exceptional insight into his world, and he sometimes suffers from skewed judgment. In turn, critics of *The Catcher in the Rye*, very much like the teachers and other figures of authority in the book, have also been both right and wrong. They have tended to overvalue Holden's insights, but have perhaps been right, after all, to treat his psychological disturbance as more normal than abnormal. The extreme verge of adolescent disturbance, after all, can be said both to approximate what would have to be diagnosed as psychosis in an adult, and to be a phase that can end in normalcy. Holden represents an extreme, but readers have sensed that he nevertheless connects with common experience.

Critics, common readers, the author of *The Catcher in the Rye* himself—all have found themselves drawn toward Holden.

Some have reasoned that their attraction could be accounted for by the universality of his case, which they have taken to be essentially that of a normal teenager. Others have reasoned that, on the contrary, he is a special case: attractive precisely to the extent that his experience is not normal. But whether one is assessing Holden's sanity or his status as a social critic, the foregoing sketch of his psychology suggests that whoever wishes to hold an informed view of Holden Caulfield needs to take into account the peculiar patterns of adolescent crisis.

Holden Caulfield Is a Teenage Everyman

Robert Coles

Robert Coles is a child psychiatrist, professor at Harvard University, and the author of more than seventy-five books, including the Pulitzer Prize-winning series Children of Crisis. *He has been awarded both the Presidential Medal of Freedom and the National Humanities Medal.*

In this essay Robert Coles writes about his interview with Anna Freud, who is considered to have founded child psychoanalysis and was Sigmund Freud's daughter. According to Coles, Anna Freud was introduced to The Catcher in the Rye *by many of her young patients, who identified with Holden Caulfield because he spoke for them. Like them, Holden is suspicious of adults, impatient with phoniness and pretension, and trying to find out what is important in life. By doing so, he hopes to find out the cause of his depression and loneliness. Coles relates that Anna Freud diagnoses Holden as having a narcissistic personality disorder.*

For many years I was lucky, indeed, to get to talk with Anna Freud, who almost single-handedly founded the discipline of child psychoanalysis. . . .

Once, in 1975, she looked back a half a century (my tape-recorder whirling), and she recalled, really, the origins of child psychoanalysis, not to mention the consequences such a development had for parents and for teachers, for film-makers and writers: "Those were exciting days, during the first quarter of this century (and now we are headed for the last quarter!). In Vienna we began to take my father's [Sigmund Freud] ideas

Robert Coles, "Anna Freud and J.D. Salinger's Holden Caulfield," *Virginia Quarterly Review*, vol. 76, Spring 2000, pp. 214–224. Copyright © 2000 by The *Virginia Quarterly Review*, The University of Virginia. Reproduced by permission of the publisher.

so seriously [that] we tried to apply them not only with the adults who came to see us, but with children. That was the heart of what Freud [so she sometimes called him] contributed to our thinking—he looked back in a [patient's] life in order to understand where it is going, and why, and in order to help change its direction. I had worked with children as a teacher, but in the 1920s I began seeing them in an office, and training or enlisting others to do so." . . .

Anna Freud's Patients Introduce Her to *Catcher*

She went on to give an extended account of the techniques of child psychoanalysis developed in those bold, break-through years—and then, abruptly, unexpectedly, made mention of a book she'd recently been reading, after hearing so much of it, over and over, from her colleagues; and very important, from her students and patients, or analysands, as she often called them: "I've been told for years about this *Catcher in the Rye*, the book, the novel with that title—I think of it, of course, as a story being told: a person is ready to catch people, save them, rescue them from some trouble they've gotten themselves into. The 'catcher' is named Holden Caulfield, we all know—but I wonder whether the story doesn't tell us about the story-teller [J.D. Salinger], though I don't like it when we in psychoanalysis do this, make guesses that turn out to be wild guesses! This young man, Holden Caulfield, is so vividly brought to the attention of the reader that it's hard not to connect him with his creator—more so, for me at least, than [is the case with] other characters, in fiction.

"I got to know this Holden Caulfield by hearsay before I met him as a reader. My analytic patients spoke of him sometimes as if they'd actually met him; they used his words, his way of speaking. They laughed as if he had made them laugh, because of what he'd said, and how he looked at things. I began to realize that they had taken him into their minds, and hugged him—they spoke, now, not only his words in the book (quotations from it) but his words become their own words (deeply felt, urgently and emphatically expressed). There were moments when I had to be the perennially and predictably pedantic listener, ever anxious, to pin down what has been spoken, call it by a [psychoanalytic] name, fit it into my 'interpretative scheme,' you could call it. I would ask a young man or a young woman who it was just speaking—him, or her, or Holden! Well, I'd hear 'me,' but it didn't take long for the young one, the youth, the teenager, to have some second thoughts! They'd be silent; they'd mull the matter over—and I wasn't surprised, again and again, to hear a quite sensible person, not out of his mind, or her mind (not 'psychotic,' as we put it in staff conferences) speaking of this Holden Caulfield as though they'd spent a lot of time with him, and now had taken up, as their very own, his favorite words, his likes and dislikes, his 'attitude,' one college student, just starting out, once termed it.

"When I asked the student, a very bright one (as he expected I would) what he meant by the word, 'attitude,' I was given a lecture that took up virtually the entire [analytic] hour, to the point that I was reprimanding myself afterwards for giving the young fellow all he needed to avoid [discussing] the important reasons he'd come to see me! But then, I smiled to myself—I realized that what I'd learned about Holden, his 'attitude,' was what this young man wanted to understand about himself: why he was so 'skeptical' (his chosen word), why he didn't give people the benefit of the doubt, why he kept to himself, because he was inclined to 'look for trouble' when he met people, was with them (his roommates, those sitting near him in the cafeteria or in a lecture hall or seminar room). I asked him, naturally, what 'trouble' he was expecting; and he hesitated for a long time, and told me he couldn't easily 'come up with any,' not to mention do so then and there on my analytic couch! He knew I'd press for examples—and then a plaintive excuse: he wanted to swear, as Holden would, but he was worried that I'd be offended, so his tongue was tied!"

In fact, sitting there with Miss Freud, I knew well what Holden had prompted that young man to want to say, to think about, remember, as he spoke his mind, gave his comments, or his "free associations," as they came to him: all the "crap" in this life, all the "goddamn" acts we observe, the statements we hear. (Now I'm using quotation marks to distance myself from those words, even as I didn't choose to mention them in front of the august, illustrious older woman with whom I was talking, and even as she was not about to get specific, speak those words as belonging to a patient, to his favorite novelist.) A moment of awkward silence—whereupon, Miss Freud, true to form, hastened to remind both of us that "there is something to be learned from this book and what it says to those who bring it into their mental life." I am quick to nod, but not all that taken with the phrase "mental life." What I feel like saying is that Salinger's slurs and swear words are not original, but are shocking, because worked so vigorously, adroitly into his lively, arresting, thoroughly enticing, embracing narration—his constant interest in addressing his reader as a "you," and his constant desire, as well, to invoke a moral (yes!) "attitude," to provoke thereby our complacent, maybe to some extent compromised, sense of who we are, what we have done (or left undone).

Holden Caulfield's Eye for Hypocrisy

There is a lot of "crap" in this "phony" world, a "goddamn" lot, so I wanted to say, linking arms thereby with Holden, and with any number of young analysands seen in this century by the likes of Miss Freud, and me and my shrink-buddies, so I hear my thoughts aver, their mode of expression deteriorating and becoming unavailable to my vocal chords. As if she saw my lips shut tight, and figured out the give-away reason, Miss

Freud observed tersely: "Holden Caulfield says what is forbidden us to say." I both agree enthusiastically (another obliging nod) and feel uneasy—well, more irritated than I want to reveal with words or bodily gestures. But I do hear myself thinking, "What the hell!"—and then I try to speak by making a critic's summary: "Salinger has Holden cut through a lot of cant—the 'phoniness' he spots all the time." I'm being heard, but myself hear nothing. I see those eyes concentrating on mine, the face that holds them as impassive as ever, the figure so imposing. I hear my voice treasuring, nourishing that word "phoniness"—as if I had myself become Holden. I want to run down the field with that word, as he did, raise that voice of mine, refer to all the "phonies" in the world, escalate to the "frauds"; but I feel my hands holding the arms of the chair that is holding me, and quickly my reflexes deliver the goods: in a carefully modulated voice I comment on a novelist's distinctive capability, his repeated intention—"he cuts through a lot of cant, Salinger does." Then, as if there is any doubt, I summon a story's protagonist as the important moral witness: "Holden has a sharp eye for the hypocrisy and duplicity of everyday life."

Now I am gulping, feeling nervous. Those two tell-tale words, "everyday life," which in Miss Freud's mind, in mine, in just about anyone's who has read Sigmund Freud's writing, have a familiar ring—I'm tempted to summon them as a part of a derivative five-word aside: "the Phoniness of Everyday Life." In my mind I had played with a celebrated book's title, come up with a precis of sorts for a celebrated novel—Freud and Salinger's Holden become joined as the observers of their fellow human beings.

Miss Freud moves us on, moves by my tongue-tied restiveness and her own struggles with Salinger's created youth, whom she now wants to approach in an appreciative manner, responsive strictly on her terms: "I think this Holden Caulfield is very much with us, because he is very much—well, he is the one who wrote of him." She is evidently aware that she has made in that sentence a rather sweeping interpretation—her pause in the middle of the assertion signaled as much, the "well" a cautionary indication that she was going to take a leap. Then, inevitably for a psychoanalyst who had distinguished herself by her reluctance to be yet another reductionist interpreter, ever prepared (gladly, triumphantly) to explain away people and events through recourse to psychological paradigms, theories, the time had come for a proper acknowledgment of uncertainty's prevalent importance: "We can never know where a writer's life has been set aside, in the pursuit of a talent's expression."

Catcher Considered as Biography

I am moved, impressed—well (to use a word) brought up short by that renunciation, so poignantly declared (with a characteristic mix of simplicity, formality, and with a penetrating idiosyncrasy of affirmation). So much for all too many explanatory or interpretive essays wrought by literary critics, biographers, psychoanalysts—the constant need to explain, unravel, account for, get to a definitive bottom of a life, a work of art. In a few seconds (almost as if she is attending her own remarks, being given pleased pause, even wonderfilled pause by them) Miss Freud tactfully moves away from the person of Salinger, from his achievement as a novelist, to the safer and surer ground of her own working experience, and out of it, her memory's sharply instructive lessons: "I've had young analysands speak to me [in her office] as if they were Holden Caulfield, and I needed badly to pay attention to them, to him through them! 'Alright,' I say to them, 'tell me what Holden wants me to know!' It's come to that, actually, a few times; I've joined with them indirectly or implicitly, in turning Holden into a real-life person—as if *The Catcher in the Rye* is a work of biography, rather than fiction. Not that fiction doesn't get us as close to the truth as biography! My father once told me when I was teaching literature [as a young woman in Vienna] that novels are the fantasies of talented people; and he did not mean to show a lack of admiration or respect with those words—quite the contrary."

Now a notable silence; the speaker lowers her head ever so slightly, if significantly—as if to pay proper respect to a most talented person whose remarks about "talented people" had just been put on the record. We try to affirm our high regard for Freud by continuing to take the novel we've been discussing seriously, with no lapse into a dismissive discussion of psychopathology. "All of us have our extended spells of fantasy," Miss Freud observes, as if we'd best keep in mind a context, of sorts, for both Holden and his creator. I fear I then slipped, pointed out how often the word "depressed" got used when Holden felt the need to characterize his state of mind. I tell Miss Freud (as if to disown any inclination on my part to call Holden "sick," an all too obvious reflexic posture for me and my kind) about the critics who have not only noted Holden's way of describing himself, but counted the number of times he uses the word "depressed," more than a dozen instances. Her response was lengthy and animated: "Of course this man was 'depressed' at times and said so to himself—though I bet if anyone had called him that, spoke the very words he'd used in his thinking about himself at certain moments, then we'd hear quite something else: an angry refutation, or a surly dismissal conveyed in an angry facial grimace! As I read the novel, I stopped a few times when I came to the word 'depressed,' and I had to think that here was another adolescent who reserved the right to call himself what he wanted—but wouldn't tolerate you or me taking such a liberty, or a critic who was observing him!"

Holden Is Trying to Learn What Matters to Him

With that remark, Miss Freud showed a second's grimace on her own face, as if she was thinking back through years of difficult, demanding clinical work—so I thought as I wondered what she would say next, and wondered, too, what I might add to her words, which had, actually, in their sum, given me considerably more to consider than I'd guessed would be the case when they first began to be given voice by the one who wanted me to hear them. Suddenly, a sigh, and then a speaker's stiffened resolve: "We have to be sympathetic to our Holdens, but I'm not sure they want that from us—I mean, they are suspicious of just about every adult they know (starting with their parents, of course, and then their teachers!) and so they're ready for all grownups who come their way, certainly including us, whose offices they enter with several chips on their shoulders! I recall a young lad I saw (he had just turned fourteen) and every exchange we had was—oh, I felt we were both working ourselves through a minefield: he was always prepared to be doubtful, even scornful, and certainly, mistrustful. I wrote those three words down for myself—they echoed through my mind as we tried to converse, session after session, and I tried to understand what was causing his quite evident (and loudly declared) annoyance with people he met at school. I thought of him (of those words!) as I read of Holden—read his remarks about himself and his schoolmates and teachers. Finally, after one especially tense discussion with that lad, I let go of myself, I think it fair to say: I guess I gave him a piece of my mind! I said that I believe we hurt ourselves, bring ourselves down, when we strike out at others all the time, dismiss them with our sharp words or not very friendly judgments, that go unexpressed, but give shape to our looks of contempt, disdain. (By the way, I'm not sure Holden would ever have let anyone speak that way to him!)"

"In any event, I kept asking myself this question: why did that lad keep returning to me in my thoughts when I met Holden Caulfield, courtesy of Mr. Salinger? In time I reminded myself (I realized!) that Holden has been very much in the thoughts of many of the adolescents I've seen [in analysis]— he's known in England as well as here [the United States] and when he comes up [in psychoanalytic sessions] I have thought to myself: yes, I know this Holden Caulfield very well, indeed; he's everyone's adolescent boy (or young man); he's trying to figure out what's important, who's important (to him!) and why; he's also trying to figure out himself, and learn what causes his moodiness, and his loneliness—a big order for anyone, even those of us who haven't been adolescents for a few decades!" . . .

Holden Is Narcissistic

Now Anna Freud noticeably perks up—and has me struck hard, stunned, by a certain forceful intensity of dislike, some of it couched, if I may use that word, in psychoanalytic speculation, theory: "I'm always being asked what I think about Holden Caulfield, once I admit I've read the book that tells of him—after being told of him by the young patient who has just asked me! I don't dare say that he's a bit bossy and impudent and brash—that he's smitten with himself, a victim of abundant narcissism, some of it out of control, driving him to be self-indulgent, to attribute that [kind of behavior] to others, rather than see it squarely in himself. It is as if, for some young people, for a time, that character in that novel has been a talisman—he signified some elusive truth about what life means, and if you keep talking about him, you'll heal your mind, settle your mind, with his help, because he's been there, where you are, presently: the voice of experience who therefore is a wise advisor. So, the point is to overlook in him what you don't want to acknowledge about yourself—a privileged vanity constantly at work. Remember, he's seeing a psychoanalyst, in a sanitarium, and he calls himself 'sick,' at the end of the book (as I had to notice and haven't forgotten!) when he is looking ahead, but still unsure where he's going and for what reason. Of course he'll elicit the interest of his young readers, who have flocked to him—often at the behest of their teachers, who spend so much of their time working with

145

young people beset by worries and confusions, and I should add, plenty of anger and bitterness: life's disappointments that come their way, for all the means their parents possess. The more I hear about Holden, the more I think of those who have enjoyed his company—and that is where I must let the matter rest: that he and his fans belong to the same club!" ...

"I believe the issue is not so much Holden's anger and melancholy ... but I repeat, the narcissism—that's the key: what in our profession we'd call a 'narcissistic personality disorder.' He's quick to turn on others, and he gives no one the benefit of the doubt, and he's always bringing everything back to himself ('self-referential' as we'd say in a clinical conference). I hesitate to overdraw the case, but there is a certain self-assurance in this young man that slips over—becomes arrogance. One young man I was seeing [in analysis] told me his friends called him 'cocky' all the time, and then he went on to associate himself with Holden Caulfield, whose name was a commonplace of my work for a while—but as you point out, there are many young people who haven't heard of him, and if he were brought to their attention they'd yawn, or look for someone else to consider interesting!"

We were getting near matters of class, of race, as they give shape to our likes and dislikes: Holden Caulfield and his Pencey Prep School, its fancy white world, readily embraced by certain of Miss Freud's patients, by a few of mine, or by my students, some of them—one or two well-to-do African-Americans, by the way: class within race. In a sense, *The Catcher in the Rye* was a prefiguration of our contemporary psychoanalytic discussion of narcissism (as Anna Freud years ago anticipated) and of the historian Christopher Lasch's book, *The Culture of Narcissism*, which summoned theoretical ideas Sigmund Freud had in mind as he attempted to understand how individuals get on with others, summoning what anticipations or apprehensions, and why. Miss Freud, in her own way, had regarded Holden as an aspect of J.D. Salinger's thinking, if not his preoccupations. She stressed several times the "significance of brotherhood" in *Catcher*, as she once or twice chose to abbreviate the novel's title, for the sake of speaking for casual convenience—though she was never altogether at a remove from interpretive reflection both serious and formal: Holden is (or is to be) a catcher; he is Caulfield—or as she put it, "calling others in the field of his life, aiming to hold them." Immediately, with some charming shyness, even nervousness, she pulled back, apologized for her "critical excess" (would that the rest of us who teach and write be given to such second thoughts, I once more caught myself thinking—the embarrassment of one's boastfulness!). Still, like Holden and like his creator and like those who are entranced by them (and by their own possibilities as they get affirmed, asserted in life) Anna Freud hopes to find coherence, give it words that "catch" the attention of others, "hold" them decisively, whatever field they "call" their own, whatever product (whether "rye" or wryness as a point of view) being grown there: "Holden and his brothers and their sister Phoebe, with their 'discontents,' as my father put it—they all seek and welcome our attention, our membership. I think Mr. Salinger had them in mind for us before he planned his famous novel they catch us, as he was caught by the idea, the story."

Holden Caulfield's Problems Are Caused by Capitalism

Carol Ohmann and Richard Ohmann

Carol and Richard Ohmann were both professors of English at Wesleyan University. Carol Ohmann is the author of Ford Madox Ford: From Apprentice to Craftsman. *Richard Ohmann was the editor of* College English *and is the author of numerous books, including* Politics of Letters.

In the following essay, Carol and Richard Ohmann provide a neo-Marxist interpretation of The Catcher in the Rye. *Neo-Marxism is based on the philosophy known as Marxism, developed in the nineteenth century by Karl Marx and Friedrich Engels. Marxism places great emphasis on the significance of class struggle throughout history. Quoting extensively from Salinger's work, the Ohmanns assert that the things that Holden Caulfield considers phony are class distinctions and meaningless social rituals. However, Holden only sees two choices: to make do with this society or escape it completely. The Ohmanns contend that the correct response, and one that Holden ignores, is to work for a better society. They argue that Salinger has written a serious critique of American middle-class life in the 1950s.*

For us, as for almost all readers, Holden's sensitivity is the heart of [*The Catcher in the Rye*], that which animates the story and makes it compelling. Events are laden with affect for Holden. He cannot speak of an experience for long in a neutral way, apart from judgment and feeling. And of course those judgments and feelings are largely negative. Not so entirely negative as Phoebe says—"You don't like *any*thing that's happening"—but this novel is first the story of a young man

Carol Ohmann and Richard Ohmann, "Reviewers, Critics, and *The Catcher in the Rye*," *Critical Inquiry*, vol. 3, Autumn 1976, pp. 15–37. Reproduced by permission of the University of Chicago Press, conveyed through Copyright Clearance Center, Inc.

so displeased with himself and with much of the world around him that his strongest impulse is to leave, break loose, move on. From his pain follows rejection and retreat.

Holden Rejects Snobbery

But what exactly is it that puts Holden out of sorts with his life? What does he reject? The critics answer . . . phrases that universalize: an immoral world, the inhumanity of the world, the adult world, the predicament of modern life, the human condition, the facts of life, evil. As we see it, the leap is too quick and too long. Holden lives in a time and place, and these provide the material against which his particular adolescent sensibility reacts.

Holden has many ways of condemning, and an ample lexicon to render his judgments. Some people are bastards, others jerks. The way they act makes you want to puke. What they do and say can be—in Holden's favorite adjectives—depressing, corny, dopey, crumby, screwed-up, boring, phony. "Phony" is probably Holden's most frequent term of abuse, definitely his strongest and most ethically weighted. For that reason his application of the word is a good index to what he finds most intolerable in his life. And Holden is quite consistent in what he calls phony.

Holden says he left Elkton Hills, one of the schools he attended before Pencey, because he was "surrounded by phonies," in particular Mr. Haas the headmaster, "the phoniest bastard I ever met in my life." Haas earned this label in the following way:

> On Sundays [he] went around shaking hands with everybody's parents when they drove up to school. He'd be charming as hell and all. Except if some boy had little old funny-looking parents. You should've seen the way he did with my roommate's parents. I mean if a boy's mother was sort of fat or corny-looking or something, and if somebody's father was one of those guys that wear those suits with very

> big shoulders and corny black-and-white shoes, then old
> Haas would just shake hands with them and give them a
> phony smile and then he'd go talk, for maybe half an *hour,*
> with somebody else's parents. I can't stand that stuff.

In a word, snobbery. Haas toadies to those who comfortably
wear the uniform of their class—some register of high bourgeois—and snubs those with padded shoulders and unfash-
ionable shoes who have come lately to their money, or not at
all. His gestures to the latter are inauthentic, and such contempt can wound. But only because class does exist: Haas is
not just personally mean; his phoniness and his power to hurt
depend on an established class system that institutionalizes
slight and injury.

Just a bit later Holden tells of another phony, an old
Pencey grad named Ossenburger who has "made a pot of
dough" through a chain of "undertaking parlors all over the
country that you could get members of your family buried for
about five bucks apiece." Holden has little respect for
Ossenburger's enterprise: "He probably just shoves them in a
sack and dumps them in the river." Nonetheless, Ossenburger
is an eminence at Pencey, to which he has given "a pile of
dough," and where Holden's dormitory is named after him.
On a football weekend Ossenburger comes to the school in
"this big goddam Cadillac," receives an obligatory cheer at the
game, and gives a speech in chapel "that lasted about ten
hours." It is a pious affair, making obliquely the Calvinist connection between wealth and virtue. Ossenburger extols prayer:

> he started telling us how he was never ashamed, when he
> was in some kind of trouble or something, to get right down
> on his knees and pray to God. . . . He said *he* talked to Jesus
> all the time. Even when he was driving his car. That killed
> me. I can just see the big phony bastard shifting into first
> gear and asking Jesus to send him a few more stiffs.

Holden demystifies in the telling, better than if he had said,
"this man claims legitimacy for his money, his Cadillac, his

business ethics, his eminence and class privilege, by enlisting religion on his side." Again, phoniness is rooted in the economic and social arrangements of capitalism, and in their concealment.

Holden Rejects Social Conventions

But a second motif in these scenes also deserves comment. The clues to phoniness lie in outward forms of conduct. Haas' phony smile follows an external convention, but accords poorly with emotional reality. His handshakes imply equality, but thinly hide the reverse of equality. Ossenburger talks within a framework of conventions: he is in chapel; he gives a sermon; he speaks of prayer. Holden's revulsion attends, in part, on ceremony itself: on prescribed forms that shape the flow of our words and movements. A smile, a handshake, a chapel assembly with boys seated in rows, a sermon, a prayer: none of these is a spontaneous expression of the self; all impose limits and bear conventional meaning. Holden resents these constraints, and delights in release from them. Hence:

> The only good part of [Ossenburger's] speech was right in the middle of it. He was telling us all about what a swell guy he was, what a hot-shot and all, then all of a sudden this guy sitting in the row in front of me, Edgar Marsalla, laid this terrific fart. It was a very crude thing to do, in chapel and all, but it was also quite amusing. Old Marsalla.

We won't offer a disquisition on old Marsalla's fart, but these things may be noted: a fart is the antithesis of ceremony (in this society, anyhow). It asserts the body, assaults manners and convention. Here, it shatters Ossenburger's hypocrisy and boastfulness. But it also strikes at the social idea behind a "*speech*" itself. It mocks the meaning of "sitting in the *row*." It is a "crude thing to do, in *chapel* and all." In brief, it is commendable ("quite amusing") because it challenges, not only Ossenburger's false ideology, but also the very existence of social forms.

These twin themes run through the book. When a situation or act seems phony to Holden, it evidences bad class relationships, or public ritual, or both. The first theme is foregrounded when Holden stigmatizes the word "grand," or the phrase "marvelous to see you"; the second when he notes the hollow formality of "glad to've met you." The first theme unites the Wicker Bar at the Seton Hotel, ambitious lawyers, the fashionable opinion that the Lunts are "angels," Spencer's deference to headmaster Thurmer, the night club set's public affection for pseudoculture (cute French songs), the "dirty little goddam cliques" at boys' schools (where "all you do is study so that you can learn enough to be smart enough to be able to buy a goddam Cadillac some day"), Andover, "Ivy League voices," men in "their goddam checkered vests, criticizing shows and books and women in those tired, snobby voices." The second theme is foregrounded in Sally Hayes' *letter*, inviting Holden to help trim the *Christmas tree*; in the black piano player, Ernie, and his "very phony, *humble*" *bow* to his philistine audience; in that audience's *applause*; in *actors'* conventional representation of people; in ministers' *sermons* ("they all have these Holy Joe voices. . . . I don't see why the hell they can't talk in their natural voice"); in Stradlater's *hello* to Ackley; in Holden's *handshake* with Ackley; in phony *parties* and smoking for show and *conversations* about art.

Holden rounds on mores and conventions that are a badge of class. He also revolts against convention itself. We would remark here that although these two feelings often blend, they have quite different origins. Society is imaginable without privilege, snobbery, unequal wealth. To banish *all* convention would be to end society itself. More of this later.

Holden Is Depressed by the Social Order

For now, we want to underline the first of the two conclusions we have reached by looking at what Holden calls phony. The novel's critique of class distinction may be found, not just between the lines of Holden's account, but in some of his most explicit comment on what's awry in his world. We must quote at some length from his digression on suitcases. When Holden meets the two nuns in the sandwich bar, their suitcases prompt him to say,

> It isn't important, I know, but I hate it when somebody has cheap suitcases. It sounds terrible to say it, but I can even get to hate somebody, just *looking* at them, if they have cheap suitcases with them. Something happened once. For a while when I was at Elkton Hills, I roomed with this boy, Dick Slagle, that had these very inexpensive suitcases. He used to keep them under the bed, instead of on the rack, so that nobody'd see them standing next to mine. It depressed holy hell out of me, and I kept wanting to throw mine out or something, or even *trade* with him. Mine came from Mark Cross, and they were genuine cowhide and all that crap, and I guess they cost quite a pretty penny. But it was a funny thing. Here's what happened. What I did, I finally put *my* suitcases under *my* bed, instead of on the rack, so that old Slagle wouldn't get a goddam inferiority complex about it. But here's what he did. The day after I put mine under my bed, he took them out and put them back on the rack. The reason he did it, it took me a while to find out, was because he wanted people to think my bags were his. He really did. He was a very funny guy, that way. He was always saying snotty things about them, my suitcases, for instance. He kept saying they were too new and bourgeois. That was his favorite goddam word. He read it somewhere or heard it somewhere. Everything I had was bourgeois as hell. Even my fountain pen was bourgeois. He borrowed it off me all the time, but it was bourgeois anyway. We only roomed together about two months. Then we both asked to be moved. And the funny thing was, I sort of missed him after we moved, because he had a helluva good sense of humor and we had a lot of fun sometimes. I wouldn't be surprised if he missed me, too. At first he only used to be kidding when he called my stuff bourgeois, and I didn't give a damn—it *was* sort of

funny, in fact. Then, after a while, you could tell he wasn't kidding any more. The thing is, it's really hard to be room-mates with people if your suitcases are much better than theirs—if yours are really *good* ones and theirs aren't. You think if they're intelligent and all, the other person, and have a good sense of humor, that they don't give a damn whose suitcases are better, but they do. They really do. It's one of the reasons why I roomed with a stupid bastard like Stradlater. At least his suitcases were as good as mine.

The source of Holden's feeling could hardly be clearer, or related with more social precision. He belongs by birthright at Elkton Hills; Dick Slagle presumably does not. Their situation—living together—calls for an equality of human beings. (School itself, the American institution that most supports our myth of equal opportunity, carries the same hope.) Likewise, Holden's desires point him toward a world in which human qualities like intelligence and a sense of humor would be the ground of relatedness, rather than Mark Cross luggage and the money that stands behind it.

Both boys are deformed by what they bring with them to their room from the social order outside. Holden is depressed, and wishes to find the right gesture (throw the suitcases away, trade with Slagle) to deny their socially imposed difference. He is hurt by Slagle's resentment, when it becomes more than kidding, and he finally gives up on the relationship. Slagle, naturally, suffers more. Shame over his suitcases is one thing. But worse are the contradictory feelings: he hates the class injustice, and strives through the word "bourgeois" ("He read it somewhere") for the ideas that would combat it; yet at the same time he longs to be on the *right* side of the barrier, to *benefit* from class antagonism by having others think he owns the Mark Cross suitcases. Clearly Holden understands all this; we can only suppose that Salinger does too.

It was the nuns' suitcases, and their straw baskets, that reminded Holden of Dick Slagle, and the nuns also stir in him reflections about money and the expression of social feeling. He tries to imagine women from his own class "collecting dough for poor people in a beat-up old straw basket," but it's "hard to picture." His aunt is "pretty charitable," but always dressed in a way that emphasizes her condescension. "I couldn't picture her doing anything for charity if she had to wear black clothes and no lipstick. . . ." As for Sally Hayes' mother: "Jesus Christ. The only way *she* could go around with a basket collecting dough would be if everybody kissed her ass for her when they made a contribution." If they didn't, she'd get bored and "go someplace swanky for lunch. That's what I liked about those nuns. You could tell, for one thing, that they never went anywhere swanky for lunch. It made me so damn sad. . . ." At the root of Holden's sadness are lives confined by poverty, the loss of human connectedness, the power of feelings distorted by class to overcome natural bonds of affinity and friendship. In the end, one chooses to room with "a stupid bastard like Stradlater," whose suitcases are as good as one's own.

So we hold that the text of this novel, and the experience of it, warrant a formulation of what wounds Holden quite a lot more precise than the one given it by phrases like "the complexity of modern life," "the neurosis and fatigue of the world," or "our collective civilized fate." These epitomes are in fact strongly ideological. They displace the political emotion that is an important part of Salinger's novel, finding causes for it that are presumed to be universal.

Likewise, the majority opinion on what Holden yearns for—ideal love, innocence, truth, wisdom, personal integrity, etc. Let's examine one such idea in detail. James Miller writes, "Perhaps in its profoundest sense Holden's quest is a quest for identity, a search for the self. . . ." Holden tries various disguises, but "the self he is led to discover is Holden's and none other. And that self he discovers is a human self and an involved self that cannot, finally, break with what Hawthorne once called the 'magnetic chain of humanity.' . . ." Miller writes of the self as if it were innate, genetically coded, yet somehow repressed. When Holden does rediscover it, it is "human" and "involved."

These rather vague characterizations lack social content. Yet we doubt that Miller or anyone else believes the identity of a person to lie beyond social influence, not to say definition. Any society provides identities for its members to step into; Holden's is no exception. We can hardly consider his quest for identity apart, for instance, from the fact that his father is a corporation lawyer ("Those boys really haul it in") on the edge of the ruling class, who has tried, however fruitlessly, to open for Holden the way to a similar identity by apprenticing him in a series of private schools. For Holden, such an identity is imaginatively real, and coercive. He gives it a reasonably concrete description when Sally Hayes refuses his invitation to go live by a brook in Vermont. She says there will be time for such pleasures later, after college. Holden:

> No, there wouldn't be. There wouldn't be oodles of places to go at all. It'd be entirely different. . . . We'd have to go downstairs in elevators with suitcases and stuff. We'd have to phone up everybody and tell 'em good-by and send 'em postcards from hotels and all. And I'd be working in some office, making a lot of dough, and riding to work in cabs and Madison Avenue buses, and reading newspapers, and playing bridge all the time, and going to the movies and seeing a lot of stupid shorts and coming attractions and newsreels.

Holden understands well enough that such an identity is incompatible with the spontaneous feeling and relatedness he wishes for.

Holden's Three Choices

But what vision can he entertain of some alternate self? Here imagination darkens. Holden has no idea of changing society, and within the present one he can see forward only to the bourgeois identity that waits for him. So he fantasizes another identity which fulfills desire by escaping society almost entirely. He would hitchhike out West to "where it was pretty and sunny and where nobody'd know me," get a (working class) job at a filling station, and build a cabin at the edge of the woods. He would "pretend I was one of those deaf-mutes," thereby ending the necessity of having "goddam stupid useless conversations with anybody." If he married, it would be to a beautiful deaf-mute, and if they had children, "we'd hide them somewhere . . . and teach them how to read and write by ourselves." No corporate structure and no Madison Avenue; but also no social production, no school, and no talk. In short, an identity for Holden that erases human history.

Here is the main equivocation of the book, and it seems to be both Holden's and Salinger's. We argued a while back that the force of Holden's severest judgment is divided. "Phony" stigmatizes both the manners and culture of a dominant bourgeoisie—class society—and ceremonies and institutions themselves—any society. As long as we listen to the critical themes of the novel, the equivocation doesn't matter much: after all, the only society around *is* bourgeois society. But when we listen to those hints in the novel of something better, of alternative futures, of reconstruction, it makes a great deal of difference. Given Salinger's perception of what's wrong, there are three possible responses: do the best you can with this society; work for a better one; flee society altogether. Only the second answers to the critical feeling that dominates the book, but Salinger omits precisely that response when he shows Holden turning from that which his heart rejects to that which has value, commands allegiance, and invites living into the future without despair. So, when Holden imagines an adult self he can think only of the Madison Avenue executive or the deaf-mute, this society or no society.

And what does he like in the present? Phoebe accuses him of not liking anything, but he likes much: his dead brother Allie, for inscribing poems on his baseball mitt; Jane Gallagher, for keeping her kings in the back row at checkers. Both violate convention, and show a disdain for winning. Richard Kinsella, who broke the rules of the Oral Expression class, and digressed upon his uncle's brace when he should have been telling about his father's farm. The nuns with their straw baskets, poor but outside competitive society. James Castle, who refused even the minimal compromise with society that would have saved his life. The Museum of Natural History, where the Eskimos remain as changeless as figures on a Grecian urn, and so defy historical process. For Holden, images of the valuable are generally images of people withdrawn from convention—people who are private, whimsical, losers, saints, dead. Holden's imagination cannot join the social and the desirable. At the beginning and again at the end of the novel he has the illusion of disappearing, losing his identity altogether—both times when he is crossing that most social of artifacts, a street.

So long as the choice is between this society and no society, Holden's imagination has no place to go. He wants love and a relatedness among equals. These do not thrive in the institutions that surround him, but they cannot exist at all without institutions, which shape human feeling and give life social form. When Phoebe retrieves Holden from nothingness and despair she draws him, inevitably, toward institutions: the family, school, the Christmas play, the zoo in the park, the carrousel where "they always play the same songs." In short, toward the same society he has fled, and toward some of its innocent social forms, this time magically redeemed by love.

Holden returns to society, the only one available. It is unchanged; he has changed somewhat, in the direction of acceptance. To go the rest of the way back, he requires the help of another institution, and a psychoanalyst. Society has classified him as neurotic—a fitting response, apparently, to his having wanted from it a more hospitable human climate than it could offer. He will change more. Society will not. But that's all right, in the end: the very act of telling his story has overlaid it with nostalgia, and he misses everybody he has told about, "Even old Stradlater and Ackley, for instance. I think I even miss that goddam Maurice. It's funny. Don't ever tell anybody anything. If you do, you start missing everybody." In a word, *Art* forms the needed bridge between the desirable and the actual, provides the mediation by which social experience, rendered through much of the story as oppressive, can be embraced.

Catcher Is a Serious Critique of Bourgeois Life in the 1950s

The Catcher in the Rye is among other things a serious critical mimesis of bourgeois life in the Eastern United States, ca. 1950—of snobbery, privilege, class injury, culture as badge of superiority, sexual exploitation, education subordinated to status, warped social feeling, competitiveness, stunted human possibility, the list could go on. Salinger is astute in imaging these hurtful things, though not in explaining them. Connections exist between Holden's ordeal and the events reported on the front page of the *Times,* and we think that those connections are necessary to complete Salinger's understanding of social reality. Iran and Korea and the hard-pressed New York school system express the hegemony of Holden's class, as do Broadway and Pencey and Stradlater. Salinger's novel makes no reference to the economic and military scope of that class's power, but the manners and institutions he renders so meticulously are those of people who take their power for granted, and expect their young to step into it.

We say, further, that these themes are not just discernible to the eye of an obsessed political reader, as one might strain to give *Catcher* an ecological or existential or Seventh Day Adventist reading. They are central to the book's meaning and to the impact it has on us and other readers. Its power is located, all agree, in Holden's sensitivity, keen observation, and moral urgency, and in the language with which he conveys these in relating his story. For all his perceptiveness, though, he is an adolescent with limited understanding of what he perceives. Readers (adults, at least) understand more, and in this gap a poignancy grows. Most readers share or are won to Holden's values—equality, spontaneity, brotherhood—but sense that these values cannot be realized within extant social forms. The novel draws readers into a powerful longing for what-could-be, and at the same time interposes what-is, as an unchanging and immovable reality.

It does so in a way that mirrors a contradiction of bourgeois society: advanced capitalism has made it imaginable that there could be enough "suitcases" for everyone, as well as spontaneity and brotherhood, and it feeds these desires at the same time that it prevents their fulfillment. Only a few can hope for suitcases and spontaneity, at the expense of the many, and enjoyment of them depends on shutting out awareness of the many. Furthermore, even the few are somehow blocked from enjoyment by the antagonistic striving required to secure one's suitcases, by the snotty human relationships of the Wicker Bar and Madison Avenue, by what Philip Slater calls "our invidious dreams of personal glory." In short, the esthetic force of the novel is quite precisely located in its rendering a contradiction of a particular society, as expressed through an adolescent sensibility that feels, though it cannot comprehend, this contradiction. Short of comprehension, both Holden and Salinger are driven to a false equation—to reject this society is to reject society itself—and a false choice—accept this society or defect from society altogether.

It is here that the novel most invites criticism, informed by history and politics. But the critics have instead, with few exceptions, followed Salinger's own lead and deepened the confusion of the novel with the help of mystifications like "the adult world," "the human condition," and so on. Pressing for such formulations, they have left history and the novel behind. They have failed both to understand its very large achievement—for we consider it a marvelous book—and to identify the shortcomings of its awareness and its art. And in this way they have certified it as a timeless classic.

Holden Caulfield's Depression Is Caused by Emotional, Not Political, Factors

James E. Miller Jr.

James E. Miller Jr. is the author of numerous books and articles on American literature, including J.D. Salinger. Miller was the editor of the journal College English.

In this viewpoint James E. Miller Jr. takes issue with Carol and Richard Ohmann's political interpretation of The Catcher in the Rye, *stating that the problems of a sensitive teenage boy cannot be solved by addressing social and political issues. Miller cites scenes from the novel to support his thesis that Holden's depression is caused by personal issues, in particular his struggle to achieve sexual maturity.*

[C]ritics Carol and Richard Ohmann define *The Catcher in the Rye*] as "a serious critical mimesis of bourgeois life in the Eastern United States, ca. 1950—of snobbery, privilege, class injury, culture as a badge of superiority, sexual exploitation, education subordinated to status, warped social feeling, competitiveness, stunted human possibility, the list could go on. Salinger is astute in imaging these hurtful things, though not in explaining them." These themes, we are told, are "central to the book's meaning and to the impact it has on us." The book's readers ("adults, at least") are "won to Holden's values—equality, spontaneity, brotherhood—but sense that these values cannot be realized within extant social forms. The novel draws readers into a powerful longing for what-could-be, and at the same time interposes what-is, as an unchanging and immovable reality."

James E. Miller Jr., "Catcher in and out of History," *Critical Inquiry*, vol. 3, Spring 1977, pp. 599–603. Reproduced by permission of the University of Chicago Press, conveyed through Copyright Clearance Center, Inc.

A Sociopolitical Reading of *Catcher* Is Simplistic

Although the Ohmanns introduce some qualifiers in these summary generalizations, their reading of *Catcher* and their view of its limitations are in reality comprehensive and exclusive. If the reader grants their generalizations, he is likely to find that other views or approaches embodying his experience of the novel are no longer tenable. A close glance at the Ohmann reading reveals it as simplistic: Holden's warm, human values are pitted against a cold, selfish society; Holden's (and Salinger's) main failure (the "confusion of the novel") is in choosing only between rejoining or dropping out from this bourgeois, capitalistic society instead of opting for radical—that is, socialist—change.

Few would want to deny a political-economic dimension to *Catcher*, and it is possibly true that this dimension has been slighted in past criticism. But to see Holden's malaise of spirit solely or even mainly caused by the evils of a capitalistic society is surely myopic; and to envision a utopian socialistic society (even were we to grant its possible creation) as miraculously erasing all the problems Holden faces is naive. The problems of a sensitive and perceptive adolescent moving painfully to maturity can never be solved by restructuring society politically and economically.

Early in the novel we hear Holden on his history teacher, "Old Spencer": ". . . you wondered what the heck he was still living for. I mean he was all stooped over, and he had very terrible posture, and in class, whenever he dropped a piece of chalk at the blackboard, some guy in the first row always had to get up and pick it up and hand it to him." We learn that Holden's brother Allie died of leukemia some years before the novel opens, and that Holden has kept his memory alive through his baseball mitt on which Allie had copied out Emily Dickinson poems. In the dormitory room next to Holden's lives the unfortunate Robert Ackley, with "lousy teeth" that "always looked mossy and awful," who had "a lot of pimples" and a "terrible personality"—a "sort of nasty guy." When Holden's roommate Stradlater refuses to tell Holden whether he made it or not with Holden's friend Jane Gallagher, Holden strikes out and is struck down, bleeding. Over and over again Holden complains that nobody ever gives your message to anybody. Over and over again we hear Holden cry out: "I felt so lonesome, all of a sudden. I almost wished I was dead."

This catalogue of characters, incidents, expressions could be extended indefinitely, all of them suggesting that Holden's sickness of soul is something deeper than economic or political, that his revulsion at life is not limited to social and monetary inequities, but at something in the nature of life itself— the decrepitude of the aged, the physical repulsiveness of the pimpled, the disappearance and dissolution of the dead, the terrors (and enticements) of sex, the hauntedness of human aloneness, the panic of individual isolation. Headlines about Korea, Dean Acheson, and the cold war seem, if not irrelevant, essentially wide of the mark—if we define the mark as the heart and soul of *Catcher*.

Holden's Sexual Maturity Is Central to the Novel

The important comic scene in which Holden is victimized by the elevator operator Maurice and the prostitute Sunny surely must be read as something more than a revelation of "sexual exploitation" in a capitalistic society. The economic-political reading of the novel tends to pass over without mention Holden's groping about in desperation to come to terms with his sexuality, which both fascinates and threatens, lures and depresses him. His sexual feelings are central to the maturing process he is undergoing, and they lie obscurely behind his tender feelings for (and secret envy of) the various children he encounters: they remain in the pre-adult world of unsullied innocence. The title of the novel itself directs attention to

Holden's dream, which he reveals to Phoebe, of standing on the edge of "some crazy cliff" near a playing field of rye, catching the kids before they fall over the cliff: the fall would surely be into sexuality, experience, adulthood.

It is difficult to see how the Marxist reading might come to terms with the crucial scene near the end of the novel, when Holden wakes up in fright to find his old and trusted teacher, Mr. Antolini, patting him on the head. Holden rushes away, to wonder later whether he had done the right thing, whether Antolini was really a "flit"—or a genuine friend in a generally hostile world. This self-questioning sets off a chain of events that brings Holden to a confrontation with his own death as he descends into the Egyptian tomb at the museum, sees again the ubiquitous obscene phrase he has rubbed off of Phoebe's school walls, and envisions his own tombstone with his name, the years of entry and exit, and the phrase pursing him into imagined death—"F--- you." It is shortly after this that Holden, refusing to agree to Phoebe's running away to the west with him, announces that he has decided to stay—to rejoin the human race. As he watches Phoebe going around and around on the carrousel, grabbing for the gold ring, he realizes that he cannot shield her from experience: "If they [the kids] fall off, they fall off, but it's bad if you say anything to them." And the action of the novel closes as Holden feels so "damn happy" that he is "damn near bawling" watching Phoebe going around and around: he has fallen and survived, and he has discovered that he can be happy in the presence of an innocence he no longer has—without being a catcher in the rye.

The Ohmanns consider that the "shortcomings of [*Catcher*'s] awareness and its art" are manifest in its failure to show that Holden had an option of working for a better society. It is not at all clear, however, that Holden refuses this option. Mr. Antolini, in one of the novel's deepest moments, quotes Wilhelm Stekel to Holden: "The mark of the immature man is that he wants to die nobly for a cause, while the mark of mature man is that he wants to live humbly for one." The comment comes at a critical turning-point for Holden, and is certainly lodged firmly in his psyche. But of course it is true that Holden does not turn his face into the sunrise at the end of the novel, expressing his determination to overthrow the bourgeois capitalistic society in favor of a socialist utopia. Indeed, the whole thrust of the novel seems to suggest that there is no social or political or economic structure that could insure sexual tranquility, banish pimples, outlaw old age, abolish death—or that would relieve Holden or any other human being of the tragic implications of his physical, sexual, emotional nature: to these he must reconcile himself, recognizing not only the "shortcomings" of man but also the "shortcomings" of himself.

But Holden is not so shortsighted, I think, as the Ohmanns suggest. In the closing lines of the novel, he confesses of the tale he has told: "I'm sorry I told so many people about it. About all I know is I sort of *miss* everybody I told about. Even old Stradlater and Ackley, for instance. I think I even miss that goddam Maurice. It's funny. Don't ever tell anybody anything. If you do, you start missing everybody." The Ohmanns consider this confession an overlay of "nostalgia." If it strikes them as naive or sentimental, it is hard to understand how they can believe so fiercely in a socialist utopia that must surely be based on some kind and measure of the human love—agape, not eros alone—Holden has attained at the end of *Catcher*. If a utopia is established without this kind of mutual love and understanding, is it not likely to turn into the kind of dictatorship with which the twentieth century is so familiar? In any event, the Ohmanns might have recognized that Holden has been awakened to a precondition of a better society—love of fellow human beings—before condemning Salinger for not instilling Holden with a vision of the kind of ideal state that has never existed before and seems not to exist now.

Would we really want Salinger to recycle the visions of [Edward Bellamy's] *Looking Backward* or [William Dean Howells's] *A Traveler from Altruria*? The experience of the twentieth century has forced the literary imagination to portray the dark underside of such bright visions—as in [Aldous Huxley's] *Brave New World* and [George Orwell's] *1984*. Holden joins a long succession of American "heroes" ([Nathaniel] Hawthorne's, [Herman] Melville's, [Henry] James', [Mark] Twain's, and more) in discovering that experience is inevitably made up of good and bad, love and hate, light and dark. The Ohmanns have censured previous critics for removing *Catcher* from history. Do they not propose at the end to carry Holden out of baffling, muddled history into a tidy and clear-cut ideology?

Contemporary Perspectives on Depression

Many Risk Factors Can Trigger Depression

Bev Cobain

Bev Cobain, an accredited psychiatric/mental-health nurse, is cousin to Kurt Cobain, the singer of the band Nirvana who committed suicide in 1994.

In the following viewpoint Bev Cobain explains how the brain works and what happens to the brain of a depressed person. She outlines several risk factors for adolescent depression, including genetics, hormonal imbalances, physical conditions, anxiety disorders, conduct problems, and being perceived as different from other teens. Cobain urges depressed teens to admit they need help and to find someone to talk to about their depression.

Depression affects your brain, which leads to mental, emotional, and even physical changes (so you might think of depression as a "whole body" or "whole being" illness). Your brain is your body's most complex organ; it's much more intricate than the most sophisticated computers. It transmits and receives information through electrical messages passed along your body's nerve pathways. Your brain produces and uses special chemicals called neurotransmitters to move these messages along the nerve cells. In fact, your brain sends *billions* of messages each second to all areas of your body with one goal: to keep you alive and healthy.

Your brain produces and stores many neurotransmitter chemicals, but three main ones have been studied in connection with depression.

Bev Cobain, From *When Nothing Matters Anymore: A Survival Guide for Depressed Teens.* Edited by Elizabeth Verdick. Free Spirit Publishing, 2007. Copyright © 1998, 2007 by Bev Cobain, R.N.,C. All rights reserved. Reproduced by permission.

These chemicals are:

- norepinephrine (NOR-ep-uh-NEHF-run),
- dopamine (DOHP-uh-meen), and
- serotonin (SEHR-uh-TOH-nun).

These three chemicals move messages to and from your brain along specialized nerve cells (called neurons) throughout your body's central nervous system. Your neurons are unique and don't look exactly like anyone else's, but they have the same basic parts, including axons and dendrites. When your brain sends a message, it travels as an electrical signal along the axon of a neuron. Between the end of one nerve cell and the beginning of another is a tiny gap known as a synapse.

The message needs to cross the synaptic gap, so the transmitting cell releases one of its chemicals (for example, serotonin). The molecules of serotonin fill the gap and attach themselves to the next cell, forming a "bridge of serotonin." The message travels across the gap, is processed by the next neuron, and continues along that cell's axon to the next gap, where more serotonin is released. This process continues until the message reaches its destination. Once the message is delivered, the serotonin has done its job and is no longer needed; it's then reabsorbed by the transmitting cell (a process called reuptake). If you don't have enough serotonin available for release into the synaptic gap, millions of messages aren't properly transmitted to the receiving cell. The disruption leads to symptoms of depression.

Imagine that the "depressed" brain is a large company (say, the Acme Rug Company) with all sorts of important functions and responsibilities. Now pretend that the company has a disabled communications center—all the different departments must try to communicate with each other over frayed and disconnected telephone wires, short-circuited lines, and cords plugged into the wrong places. What happens? The departments can't communicate or get anything done. If you're depressed, your brain (like the imaginary Acme Rug Company) can't communicate properly—important messages to your body are simply lost in transmission.

When Your Brain and Body Stop "Talking"

Why does depression affect your brain, body, moods, and behavior—everything about you? Because when you're depressed, your brain and body can't work together well enough to help you function normally. Your body depends on your brain to tell it to eat, drink, sleep, move, and feel. When your brain and body stop "talking," you're unable to process these important messages (it's like your brain is giving you the "silent treatment").

Your brain's limbic system helps regulate your emotions and your motivation. It's made up of several different areas, each responsible for certain tasks. Here are some examples:

- The *thalamus* screens and sorts messages from your senses (sight, smell, touch, hearing, and taste). If your thalamus doesn't receive the messages correctly, one result might be that foods don't look, smell, or taste appealing.

- The *hypothalamus* is the source of your feelings, including your sexual feelings; it also controls your blood pressure and tells you when you're hungry and thirsty. If your hypothalamus is impaired, you may feel hungry a lot, lose your appetite, or have an increased (or decreased) interest in sex.

- The *amygdala* can activate anger and aggression, or make you feel calm, depending on the part that's stimulated. Overstimulation or understimulation of the amygdala may cause problems with anger and self-control.

- The *hippocampus* forms and stores new memories. If your hippocampus isn't working properly, you may have trouble learning new things or remembering what you've learned.

- The *Reticular Activating System (RAS)* alerts your brain that messages are coming from the five senses, then helps you concentrate by filtering this input. If this function fails, it may be hard for you to focus. The RAS is also responsible for regulating sleep (sleep disturbances are the #1 complaint of depressed people).

- The *cerebellum* is responsible for posture, balance, and muscle coordination. If messages aren't transmitted properly in this area, you might have difficulty playing sports or just doing normal daily activities.

- The *cerebrum*, the largest part of your brain, does the "thinking" jobs like solving problems, making decisions, and receiving, storing, and retrieving memories. Your intellect, language skills, and ability to understand numbers and the alphabet are all based in your cerebrum. If the nerve cells in your cerebrum aren't functioning well, you may not be able to think clearly, use good judgment, or communicate effectively with other people.

In fact, when you're depressed, normal functions like eating, sleeping, walking, thinking, feeling, and remembering may seem like monumental tasks.

The Causes of Depression

Experts have different opinions about what causes depression. Many believe, for example, that depression is a result of chemical imbalances in the brain. Other experts say that your genes, environment, or coping skills play a big role in whether you get depressed. Most likely, depression is the result of a combination of factors.

Many times teenagers suffer from depression, which can be caused by genetics, hormonal imbalances, or even anxiety disorders. Teens can prevent depression by admitting their condition and seeking someone to talk to—such as a counselor. © Bubbles Photolibrary/ Alamy.

Hormones, like neurotransmitters, carry messages between your nerve cells and your brain. Your hormones are responsible for transporting information that affects the growth and development of your body. If you're depressed, you might have abnormal hormone levels—specifically, levels of the hormone cortisol, which is produced in response to stress or fear.

If you're a girl, you're probably familiar with PMS (premenstrual syndrome), which can happen when your hormone levels are higher during the week before your period. The excess hormones might make you feel irritable, anxious, emotional, and out of control—depressed, in other words. Girls and women who have given birth have high hormone levels afterward, and this can lead to a form of depression known as post-partum depression.

Other physical conditions can contribute to depression, too. For example, if you have an eating disorder (such as anorexia nervosa, bulimia, or compulsive overeating disorder),

173

you're more prone to depression. If you have a chronic illness—lupus, epilepsy, arthritis, asthma, etc.—you may be dealing with physical and emotional symptoms that are painful and hard to handle, which can cause depression.

If you've been diagnosed with depression before (a "prior episode"), you may be more likely to get it again. According to Dr. Boris Birmaher, a psychiatrist at the University of Pittsburgh Medical Center, "Each episode of depression may change some biological mechanism in the brain and trigger *more* depressions. This is referred to as 'the kindling phenomenon.'" Just as kindling helps start and spread a fire, a prior episode of depression can spark future depressions.

The genes your parents passed to you can play a part in whether you're at risk for depression. Studies have shown that relatives of people with depression are two to three times more likely to suffer from it themselves. In other words, you may inherit a "genetic vulnerability." But just because you have a genetic risk doesn't automatically mean you'll become depressed.

Other risk factors for depression include:

- *A "perceived difference,"* such as obesity, a physical disability, a learning disability, or homosexuality. Because you may seem and feel "different," you might have low self-esteem and be teased by others, which can contribute to depression.

- *Anxiety disorders,* such as excessive worrying, obsessive-compulsive disorder, or panic disorder. These problems can increase your risk of depression, and they may even make your symptoms more severe and long-lasting.

- *Conduct problems* like temper tantrums, shoplifting, or skipping school. If acting out is a result of depression and you're punished for your "bad behavior," you may feel guilty, angry, or worthless—this can increase your depression.

- *Being gifted and talented.* You might assume that you have "enough smarts" to handle any emotional difficulties, so you might hold in your feelings instead of talking about them. Anyone—high IQ or not—can suffer from depression. It's okay to admit that you have a problem and need help. . . .

What Your Environment Has to Do with Depression

Experts believe there's a connection between "stressors" (things that cause stress) and teen depression. Although stressors don't necessarily cause depression, they may *trigger* it, especially if you have other risk factors for the illness. Environmental stressors occur outside you—within your home, school, or community. Examples of stressors include divorce, peer pressure, sexual or physical abuse, violence, and poverty.

The stressors may be out of your control, but you *can* learn to control how you react to them. Say, for example, that you flunk an important test at school. How do you react? Do you: (A) feel disappointed for a few days, get support from a parent or friend, then recover and move on? Or (B) feel like a total failure, keep your disappointment to yourself, and become overwhelmed by your painful feelings? If you chose A, you probably have good coping skills and a network of friends and family members who offer support when you need it. Your coping skills can help protect you from depression.

But what if you chose B? You might have a poor opinion of yourself (low self-esteem) and may have a hard time coping with painful events. Maybe you don't think your family, friends, and teachers are supportive—maybe there's no one you feel comfortable talking to. If this sounds like you, you may be at risk for depression. Holding your feelings inside—especially anger, sadness, and disappointment—can make you feel like you have no control over your life or what happens to you. When you feel powerless to change your life, you're at a higher risk for depression.

Other stressors include:

- losing a beloved person, animal, or possession
- a drop in your self-esteem
- family conflict (especially if it's frequent)
- financial problems (your own or your family's)
- the letdown after achieving a goal (a feeling of "Now what?")
- any unwelcome change in your life (including the onset of puberty)
- physical, mental, or sexual abuse (current or past).

What do all these events have in common? A sense of loss. Whether it's the loss of a loved one's presence, the loss of family harmony, or the loss of pride in yourself, you may feel like your life has changed for the worse. No matter how good your coping skills are, this kind of grief can affect you profoundly, and you may feel you have nowhere to turn. Maybe your parents or other family members don't know how to deal with emotional issues themselves and aren't offering you much support.

Family troubles often trigger depression or make it worse. If you're a depressed teen living in a home where there's conflict or abuse, you'll probably have more episodes of depression than other teens. If your family is troubled, you may feel like you can't express your emotions or concerns, or that you lack support. You may feel you're at the mercy of your environment and are helpless to change things.

It's scary to reach the limit of what you can handle. You may feel that no one understands you or cares about you—or has ever felt the same way you do. When you reach this point, you may not know how to cope anymore. If you use negative coping behaviors, like numbing yourself with drugs and/or alcohol, your depression will only worsen. If you withdraw from family and friends, you're putting more of a burden on yourself because you're shutting out people who might be able to help you.

The best thing you can do for yourself is:

1. Admit you need help.

2. Reach out and trust someone.

If you don't have a supportive family, finding a trusted adult may be difficult, but not impossible. You can talk to a teacher, your principal, your school counselor, your school social worker, a clergy member, or a family friend. Give yourself permission to cry, get angry, or be afraid—this helps you release your feelings and puts you in a better position to deal with them.

Take a look at what's going on in your life right now:

• Have you experienced a loss recently?
• Do you lack a network of people you can turn to for support?
• Are you suffering from low self-esteem?
• Do you have a family history of depressive illness or abuse?

Once you're aware of your risk factors, you can begin to understand the reasons behind your depression. It's not your fault if you're depressed—it's no one's fault. You didn't *ask* to have depression, but if you do, you need to ask for help. Your mind and body need—and deserve—to get better.

An Inability to Communicate Feelings Puts Teenage Boys at Risk of Depression

Ellen McGrath

Ellen McGrath is a clinical psychologist and chair of the American Psychological Association Task Force on Women and Depression. Among her books is When Feeling Bad Is Good.

The rate of depression and anxiety disorders is rising dramatically among teenage boys, reports Ellen McGrath, a nationally recognized expert on depression. She contends that many stressors are contributing to these increases, but that the most significant factor is adolescent males' inability to communicate their feelings. Because communicating is a vital survival skill, boys need to address this lack if they are to have successful relationships in life. McGrath offers a number of suggestions to help boys overcome an inability to communicate.

They're young, they're often highly visible—and they're in deep trouble. America's adolescent boys may look strong as they swagger down the street, but in reality they are the population at highest risk today for all kinds of serious problems.

Rates of anxiety disorders and depression are soaring among them. For the first time, depression among males is nearly as prevalent as among females in this group.

Teenage Boys Face Many Stressors

Adolescent males find themselves facing a set of unique pressures. Shifting gender opportunities have left many boys in the

Ellen McGrath, "Teen Depression—Boys: Adolescent Males Face a Unique Set of Pressures," *Psychology Today*, May 21, 2007. Reproduced by permission.

dust. The girls may now be equal players on the soccer team, but the boys no longer know the rules of play.

Then too, the boys, as well as their sisters, belong to the first generation of divorce. Instead of a stable and supportive family base to keep them from feeling overwhelmed at times of stress, many are the products of absentee parents and conflict.

And today's boys are facing unprecedented stresses from many directions. While there is less certainty about the outcome of the college race, there is no let up in expectations for male success. There is more career confusion, and paths seem less clear.

Given the disquietude, substance abuse is an easy lure, as is the pressure for early sexual activity. Contrary to popular mythology, boys are just as anxious and confused about sex as the girls are.

But perhaps the biggest problem with today's young males is that they often have mild to moderate alexithymia—they are unable to identify their own (and others') feelings and thus unable to communicate about them. They never learned how from absent or overworked fathers.

However, the ability to communicate feelings is an increasingly important survival skill. It is certainly required for stable interpersonal relationships throughout life—at school, at work, and in the families most expect eventually to create.

For adolescent boys as for anyone, resolving the pressures in one's life involves figuring out how you feel. Alexithymia is like having a padlock on your tongue.

How to Help Teenage Boys Communicate

There is an immediate need to take action. If not, our sons face life-threatening consequences—drug and/or alcohol addiction, self-destructive behavior and accidents, suicide, and violence towards others. Such problems are already rampant.

An increase of depression and anxiety disorders can be seen in teenage boys in society today. One way to cope with depression is for teenage boys to communicate their feelings of depression to others to avoid further complications in the future. Matthew Naythons/Time & Life Pictures/Getty Images.

- Educate yourself about the psychology of boys. Read Real Boys by William Pollack, Ph.D. And if you need more, get *Real Boys' Voices*, in which boys confide how they are struggling with their masculinity, their sexuality, their future, their harassment from other boys, their feelings, their relationships with their parents and girlfriends, and more.

- Talk with adolescent boys. Let them know that you're really interested in understanding their experience in the world. Make no attempt to judge the information or control the discussion.

- Discard the prevailing cultural myth that would have you take a step back from their lives. More than ever, adolescence is a time when kids need your support. Their lives depend on it.

- Recognize that there is an all-important difference in the way genders display distress. Boys tend to express negative feelings in violence toward themselves or others, in self-destructive behavior and recklessness, and in substance abuse.
- Take on the task of teaching emotional intelligence. You can't leave its development to chance. But even before you begin, tell the truth—that feelings are good, a source of strength, not a sign of weakness.

Help the young males in your life to develop an emotional vocabulary. To do this, they need to understand their own feelings and those of others, and put names to what they too often feel as undifferentiated distress.

How to Help Teenage Boys Manage Their Emotions

Then impart emotional management skills. Boys in particular need to learn how to manage stress and the negative emotions—anger, fear, frustration, sadness, loneliness, doubt—because they are at risk for acting them out.

- Teach empathy. Help boys learn to put themselves in the other person's place.
- Help boys learn to handle competitive feelings. Males especially need strengthening of the ego so they can be more independent of others' judgment when others are being negative towards them.
- Teach boys to connect and communicate instead of detaching when they face problems. Interaction always leads to better solutions. Boys need to be openly told that the closer they are to others, the safer and stronger they will feel. Support them in developing a "family of choice," composed of friends and parents of friends. And encourage them to improve relationships in their own family.

- Instruct males to ask for feedback. They need to ask others how they are coming across. The world is too complicated for anyone to figure these things out alone.

- Stay connected to young boys even though society pulls you in the other direction. My 13-year-old son occasionally asks me to walk him to school. I wouldn't think of saying no. But he consciously knows he's going to get flack from his peers. So a block from school he invariably says to me, "OK, Mom, now it's time for us to detach." We disengage our hands—but we still discuss what it all means.

Many Children Are Not Treated for Their Depression

Marianne D. Hurst

Marianne D. Hurst is a reporter and researcher for Education Week.

Marianne D. Hurst reports that between 5 and 11 percent of school-age children are suffering from depression and that experts believe only one-third of these children are treated for the condition. While there is a growing awareness that schools can play a role in screening for depression, Hurst points out that there are significant barriers to establishing school-based mental-health programs. Among these risks, she explains, is the possibility for misdiagnosis and consequently placing children on antidepressants that could potentially harm them.

He'd always been a cautious and somewhat anxious child. And because he suffered from mild cerebral palsy, the doctors already had concerns about his social-emotional welfare even when he was a toddler. But no one suspected the depth of the problem that would manifest itself in 1st grade.

Initially, the Connecticut boy had danced off to kindergarten, eager and excited. But as time passed, he developed phobias, started muttering to himself frequently, pulled out his hair until he developed a bald spot, and sometimes became too anxious to leave the house.

By 1st grade, he was having a hard time going to school. He withdrew from other children, refused to go to friends' parties, and became so fearful that he actually locked his mother out of the car one day when she tried to drop him off at school.

Despite reassurances both in the classroom and at home, his anxiety increased daily as did his tendency to worry and act out. Then, on what his mother recalls as an "awful afternoon," he simply refused to get on the school bus. He stood by the curb, crying hysterically.

The boy was suffering from childhood depression. But making that diagnosis for many youngsters can be tricky, because little research has been done on depression in preschool- and elementary-age children.

The topic is starting to gather more interest in the education community, however, in response to concerns that children suffering from depression tend to do poorly in school. And a growing body of research documents the prevalence of depression in adolescents.

"There are kindergartners and 1st graders who experience depression," says Kathie Halbach Moffitt, the project director for the depression-education project at the University of Connecticut health center in Farmington. "This can start very early."

A Significant Percentage of Children Have Depression

Overall, it is estimated that nearly 19 million adults in the United States suffer from depression. While research on the number of school-age children with depression varies, most experts agree that between 5 percent and 11 percent of 6- to 17-year-olds are living with the problem every day. Of those, experts say about two of three receive no treatment for the disease.

"It's a big problem," says Jerald Newberry, the executive director of the health-information network for the 2.7 million-member National Education Association [NEA] and a former psychologist for the 160,000-student Fairfax County schools in Virginia. "When we meet with our members to ask about the problems they face, [mental-health issues are] always number one or two."

Depression is characterized by a number of symptoms, including persistent sadness, irritability, loss of appetite, feelings of hopelessness or worthlessness, lack of concentration, and poor sleeping patterns. There can be other symptoms too, which are harder to pinpoint and often manifest themselves differently depending on age and environment.

Experts say many students suffering from depression also suffer in the classroom because they lack the motivation to learn, are hypersensitive to criticism, and may not have the self-esteem to appreciate even small achievements.

But depression, they caution, can't always be seen through failing grades. Some depressed students can be extremely gifted and show no academic signs of failure. In fact, they try to cope with their troubled feelings by becoming perfectionists or overachievers—tactics that can lead to major emotional meltdowns when youngsters do not achieve perfection. In 2000, the U.S. surgeon general issued a groundbreaking report that concluded that one out of every five children in this country has a mental-health problem, and that between 10 percent and 15 percent of children and adolescents have some symptoms of depression.

Yet even with ongoing research and a strong advertising campaign by pharmaceutical companies to raise public awareness of the availability of medications to treat depression, the disease still goes relatively undiagnosed in children, authorities on the problem say. For instance, a report released [in 2004] by the Annenberg Foundation Trust, based in Sunnylands, Calif., found that only 46 percent of physicians who treat adolescents felt confident diagnosing depression in adolescents, and only half regularly screened teenagers for mental-health problems.

However, some experts warn that numbers on depression can be deceiving, especially those that estimate the percentage of children who have the disease. Many research studies, they say, are conducted on small groups and have severe limitations. A 2002 report by the Arlington, Va.-based American Psychiatric Institute for Research and Education, for instance, found that two surveys—the National Institute of Mental Health Epidemiologic Catchment Area Program and the National Comorbidity Survey—which are often cited to substantiate the growing need for mental-health treatments for adults, overstate the scope and severity of the problem.

"There's a tendency for people to think that these numbers mean that all [depressed] kids have severe depression, the kind that leads to suicide," says Rusty Selix, the executive director of the Mental Health Association of California. "But that's not true. The numbers have validity, but you need to look at what the numbers are really telling you, and remember that not all depressive disorders have the same level of severity."

While the Connecticut mother was clearly concerned about her son's anxiety, it surprised her when he was diagnosed with depression in 1st grade. Depression, a problem all too commonly associated with adolescence, seemed impossible in a child his age, she recalls. The boy is now 13. . . .

But the National Institute for Mental Health reports that large-scale studies suggest that 2.5 percent of children under 12 run the risk of experiencing a depressive episode. Researchers say a depressive episode generally lasts seven to nine months.

Moreover, once children experience depressive episodes, experts say, more than 70 percent relapse within five years. Children with depressed parents are also three times more likely to experience depression than youngsters whose parents do not suffer from it.

Barriers to Screening for Depression in Schools

Many students could benefit from school-based mental-health programs that screen for depression, advocates of such services say. But significant barriers block the way.

To begin with, authorities say, school psychologists and counselors simply don't have enough time to tackle the issue, because they spend so much time testing students with disabilities for learning problems, rather than working with students in general.

In addition, financial limits have led districts to cut counselors and school psychologists out of their budgets, forcing many schools to make do with part-time counselors only. Even in districts that do maintain full-time positions, many counselors serve only as academic advisers—finding their roles constrained by time, caseloads, or administrators' fears about the possible legal and financial ramifications of dealing with mental-health issues.

Critics of such programs question not only their cost, but also what they see as their encroachment on parents' turf. In 1999, Karen Holgate, the president of the Parent National Network, a California-based organization for parental rights, launched a campaign against Assembly Bill 1363, a school health-care bill that would have expanded school-based health clinics throughout California. Then-Gov. Gray Davis vetoed the bill.

Among other complaints, Holgate contended that the bill would limit parental consent by offering easy-access care, health screenings, and referrals based on students' own requests. And to maintain student privacy and confidentiality, she says, the bill could have kept documentation collected in such clinics out of the hands of parents.

In papers she posted on the Internet, Holgate sharply criticized the growing belief that school-based health centers could be used effectively to treat depression and prevent school violence. The effort was a misguided attempt at the "medicalization of schools," she argued.

The Connecticut mother, as her surprise faded, began to acknowledge similarities she and her son shared. She also suffers from depression, and, as a youngster, she too had been persistently fearful, sad, and preoccupied. Her condition went virtually unnoticed by those around her, in part because she did well in school and didn't have any noticeable problems. "People with depression are different," she says. "You know that you're not normal on some level. You have to put up a good face to survive.

"Before I knew that there was a reason why I felt the way I did," she continues, "I'd see regular people doing regular things—watch them get enjoyment out of simple things—and I'd wonder, how do they do it? Why do they do it when the world is so hard?"

It took her many years, she says, to understand why other people seemed so positive in what to her was a cruel and unforgiving world. Her son's anxiety made more and more sense, and she desperately wanted to help him avoid the years of suffering she had endured.

The Connecticut boy spent his first year of therapy talking out his problems with a psychologist.

"[Depression] is such a serious, lifelong, life-altering illness," his mother says. "It affects one physically, emotionally, and spiritually. Even when you know what depression is, it's hard to conquer. And for kids, it's even more baffling because they don't have any point of reference."

Yet despite the weekly therapy sessions, the boy's worrying did not ebb. His mother utilized every avenue of cognitive therapy, but it soon became clear that talking wasn't enough. He needed medication in addition to emotional support.

Use of Antidepressants for Children Is Controversial

Of the 157 million prescriptions issued for antidepressants in 2002, about two percent were for children ages one to 11, and five percent were for adolescents ages 12 to 17, according to the U.S. Food and Drug Administration [FDA]. Still, many critics voice concern that school-based mental-health programs might add to society's increasing tendency to medicate children at the first sign of a problem, rather than trying other approaches.

Marla Filidei, the vice president of the Los Angeles-based Citizens' Commission on Human Rights, a nonprofit group that investigates violations in the psychiatry field, argues that the placement of mental-health staffing and services in schools poses a grave risk to otherwise healthy children. Many students, she says, could be misdiagnosed by "subjective testing" that has little scientific backing.

The students would then be placed on drugs that they might not need, and that could be potentially harmful to them.

For instance, Filidei points out that Paxil, a commonly prescribed antidepressant and one of a number of drugs currently under review by the FDA, was recently banned in the United Kingdom for use with children under 18. An FDA report released last week [in January 2004] questioned the effectiveness of antidepressant use on children, and raised concerns about the potential risk of an increase in suicides for children using such drugs. Critics who argue that antidepressants are overused say the report supports their arguments.

"Clinical depression—what does that mean?" Filidei says. "They're using a subjective list of criteria that can be very loosely interpreted to put 12- and 13-year-olds on drugs. It's criminal, quite honestly."

Another potential problem, she says, is the failure of some schools to inform parents about the screening process and the potential risk factors involved in medicating children.

So what is a school's role in identifying and treating childhood depression? It's a frustrating question for many school psychologists and counselors faced with an already daunting list of challenges.

"You can't tell children to leave depression at the schoolhouse door," Newberry of the NEA says. In the long run, he adds, ignoring the issue is likely to have far-reaching consequences because depressed children tend to become depressed adults.

Others echo his sentiments.

"If it were handled early, we could snap that cycle," says Erika Karres, a retired teacher who taught grades 7–12 in Orange County, N.C., for 30 years, and is a strong advocate for school-based mental-health programs. "Teachers need to be aware that 20 percent of any student body will have depression," she says. "Awareness doesn't cost any money."

Many administrators, though, are reluctant to initiate programs because of the potential social, financial, and legal ramifications. Inconsistent local funding is a problem, and there are no national standards for school-based mental-health care.

"The necessity just hasn't been impressed upon school leaders," says Karres, referring to attentiveness to students' depression. "Especially now when everything deals with achievement. . . . [But school administrators need] to understand that depression affects achievement."

The Connecticut mother agrees.

"Depression just doesn't grow out of nothing," she says. "There's a source, but the behaviors often come across as defiant. It's not recognized as depression. [The children] are saying something to you when they act like that, . . . but instead of seeing what the behavior is saying, we punish it."

The Transition to High School Increases the Potential for Depression

Barbara M. Newman, Philip R. Newman, Sarah Griffen, Kerry O'Connor, and Jayson Spas

Barbara M. Newman and Philip R. Newman have both been professors in the Department of Human Development and Family Studies at the University of Rhode Island. The Newmans are coauthors of a number of books, including Theories of Human Development. *Jayson Spas is a clinical psychologist at the University of Rhode Island. Sarah Griffen and Kerry O'Connor were participants in the research of the Department of Human Development and Family Studies.*

This essay reports the results of research to support the hypothesis that the transition to high school is a time when an adolescent's social support system diminishes, increasing the potential for symptoms of depression. Three types of support were analyzed in the research—family, peer, and school belonging—and the responses of the study's subjects (205 eighth- and ninth-grade students) supported the hypothesis of the researchers. The authors conclude that strategies to increase a sense of school belonging should be adopted during the eighth-grade year in an effort to reduce depression in adolescents.

For many adolescents, high school is a long-awaited change in status, accompanied by new freedoms and new challenges. Nonetheless, the transition to high school is often associated with negative outcomes including poorer attendance, declines in grades, newly emerging discipline problems, and

Barbara M. Newman, Philip R. Newman, Sarah Griffen, Kerry O'Connor, and Jayson Spas, "The Relationship of Social Support to Depressive Symptoms During the Transition to High School," *Adolescence*, vol. 42, Fall 2007, pp. 441–459. Copyright © 2007 Libra Publishers, Inc. Reproduced by permission.

new feelings of alienation or social rejection. Efforts to account for these changes typically focus on school size, greater anonymity, more challenging academic work, changes in the rule structure, and less adult monitoring. Increasing attention is being paid to the sense of school belonging or connectedness as a factor that contributes to success in this transition. However, few studies have examined the changes in social support that occur between the 8th and 9th grade and their impact on high school adjustment. The current study considers three sources of social support—family, peers, and school belonging—each of which could be disrupted or enhanced in the transition to high school. Two basic questions guide this research. First, what are the changes in the social support system in the transition to high school? Second, what is the relationship between each source of social support and adjustment, especially depressive symptoms? . . .

Support Systems Disrupted in Transition to High School

We conceptualize the transition to high school as a time when the adolescent's social support system is potentially disrupted and reorganized. The three primary sources of social support—family, peers, and school adults—are each likely to undergo changes as a result of the developmental transitions of adolescence combined with the transition to high school.

Family. Parent support is the paramount social support system during adolescence. [Research shows that more] than any other support system, it is directly related to an adolescent's academic success, positive self-image, self-esteem, self-confidence, and overall mental health. Parent involvement is meaningfully associated with school achievement and emotional adjustment during high school. Family support is optimal when it combines age-appropriate expectations for autonomy and closeness. . . . [Research has found] that supportive relationships with parents were associated with higher levels of emotional autonomy. . . . [Parents] who fostered both a tolerance for intimacy and individuality positively aided their children in the transition to junior high school as shown by increases in self-esteem and more positive attitudes about school. [A study published in 2000 by Barbara M. and Philip R. Newman and others] found that among a group of low-income, urban minority youth, those whose immediate and extended family members provided support, monitoring, and school engagement were more likely to sustain their academic motivation and do well. However, in the transition to high school, adolescents spend less time with their family members. They are likely to experience new family conflicts about issues related to homework, friends, the use of time and money, and personal preferences. Parental expectations for new levels of autonomy and self-sufficiency may be accompanied by a loss of intimacy and closeness.

Peers. The transition to high school can be especially difficult as adolescents shift from being the oldest and most physically mature in their school, to the youngest and least physically developed among their peers. Peer group structures from middle school are disturbed as students move to larger high schools where students regroup into new cliques and crowds. Ability grouping and academic tracking may bring students into contact with new peers and make it difficult to find time to interact with former middle school friends. [K.] Isakson and [P.] Jarvis found that "increased emphasis on social interactions creates an environment where fitting in and belonging serves as an added source of pressure." Difficulties in establishing and maintaining positive peer relationships are associated with multiple negative developmental outcomes including loneliness, school dropout, internalizing symptoms, aggression, criminality, and substance use. Peer relationships serve a variety of functions including self-validation and ego support, intimacy and affection, guidance and assistance, reliable alliance, and companionship and stimulation. Although peer relationships have a propensity to change over time and are shorter in duration than family relationships, research indicates that close friendships may be especially important for sustaining a sense of belonging and an essential factor in reducing the likelihood of depression.

School belonging. In the context of the transition to high school, adolescents lose familiar teachers, coaches, advisors, and routines. High schools are typically more anonymous settings than middle schools; they are typically larger buildings with more students in larger classes. As a consequence, high school students receive less individualized attention from teachers.

[C.] Goodenow found that an adolescent's sense of school belonging was positively associated with motivation for school, effort, level of participation, and eventual achievement in school. [G.G. Wehlage states] "school belonging means more than attendance and dropout rates; it means that students have established a social bond between themselves and the adults in the school, and the norms governing the institution." The sense of school connectedness is associated with several key features, especially the opportunity to have meaningful input into school policies, participation in class material that engages students' interest, and opportunities to engage in meaningful interactions with adults, both inside and outside the classroom. This last component, which is especially relevant to the notion of social support, reflects students' perceptions that their teachers are willing to take time to help them, that the teacher is emotionally available, that the teacher knows the student in more than a peripheral way and does not impose his or her adult status unnecessarily in order to control the student. One assumes that through relationships with teachers and other school adults, adolescents establish a sense of school belonging and internalize the norms and values of the school as a social institution. . . .

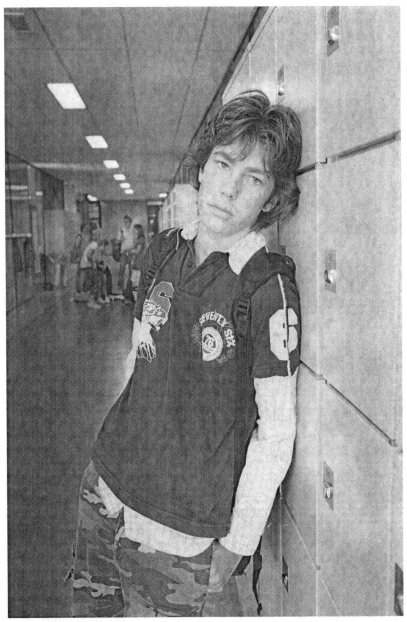

Symptoms of depression increase when a teenager makes the transition to high school—one may feel uncomfortable and alone in the new school environment. © age fotostock/ Superstock.

Disruptions in Social Support Contribute to Depression

This study examines changes in social support over the transition to high school and the relationship of social support to depression. The study complements a growing body of research that focuses on the risks for internalizing problems in early adolescence. A premise of the study is that in the transition to high school, disruptions in social support help account for increases in depressive symptoms. The study brings three unique perspectives to this problem. First, it considers social support as a multifaceted construct, including support from parents, peers, and school adults. Second, the study incorporates a design which allows a comparison of cross-sectional and longitudinal analyses of the patterns of change from 8th to 9th grade. Third, the study focuses on one school system in which all the 8th graders attend a single 9th grade, removing the potential variability among high school environments from this analysis.

The results confirm that the transition to high school is accompanied by a decline in a sense of school belonging and an increase in depressive symptoms. The results for 9th graders also indicate that parent support and school belonging are significantly associated with depressive symptoms. . . .

The high school transition is an especially sensitive period when adolescents are seeking to establish meaningful experiences of group identity and belonging. The satisfaction of belongingness needs is associated with positive outcomes while deprivation or disruption of these relationships is associated with negative outcomes. The results of this study suggest that parents, peers and schools play key roles in sustaining adolescents' sense of well-being during this transition. High schools clearly serve more than an academic function. They offer a context through which adolescents experience a sense of group belonging. Disruption of this sense of belonging or connectedness has implications for mental health, physical health, and academic achievement. . . .

One reason to be concerned about the decrease in school belonging is its link to depression. Mental health professionals are increasingly troubled about the rising incidence of depression in adolescence and its comorbidity with risky health behaviors, poorer school performance, and social isolation. Depression in early adolescence has been found to have long-term consequences for mental health problems. Future research might focus more specifically on students who report low parent support and a low sense of school belonging, and those who have experienced declines in parent support and peer support from 8th to 9th grade, since they are likely to be at greater risk for problems in school performance and mental health. Prevention and intervention efforts need to incorporate targeted efforts to enhance experiences of school belonging given the important role that connection to school appears to play in 9th graders' emotional well-being.

One of the implications of this research for intervention is the need to find innovative ways to enhance a sense of school belonging during 9th grade. Typical strategies that take place during the 8th grade year, such as a visit to the high school or a shadowing day, may need to be supplemented with new, meaningful roles and relationships once students enter the high school that will foster a greater sense of belonging. These strategies could connect 9th-grade students with adults and older students, and assign them significant tasks that contribute to the life of the high school. At the same time, high school teachers and counselors need to collaborate with parents and other family members to ensure that family support for adolescents is not disrupted during this time. New efforts are needed to evaluate those aspects of high school reform that are addressing the social and emotional needs of students to determine their impact on students' sense of school belonging and their related network of family and peer support.

Young and Depressed

Pat Wingert and Barbara Kantrowitz

Pat Wingert is Washington correspondent for Newsweek, *and Barbara Kantrowitz is a contributing editor for* Newsweek. *They are the authors of* Is It Hot in Here? Or Is It Me? The Complete Guide to Menopause.

In the following selection, Pat Wingert and Barbara Kantrowitz report that the National Institute of Mental Health estimates that 8 percent of adolescents and 2 percent of children have symptoms of depression. Some refer to a depression "epidemic" in this age group. However, it is not known if depression is becoming more common among teens or if there is simply a greater awareness of the problem. The authors write that there are difficulties in identifying depressed teens and finding the right help for them. Some depressed teens are misdiagnosed as moody, or as suffering from mononucleosis or chronic-fatigue syndrome. Once teens are diagnosed, finding the right treatment can be difficult. There is some evidence from studies to support behavioral therapy combined with drugs such as Prozac and Paxil. However, the authors claim, that combination only works in 60 percent of all cases.

Brianne Camilleri had it all: Two involved parents, a caring older brother and a comfortable home near Boston. But that didn't stop the overwhelming sense of hopelessness that enveloped her in ninth grade. "It was like a cloud that followed me everywhere," she says. "I couldn't get away from it." Brianne started drinking and experimenting with drugs. One Sunday she was caught shoplifting at a local store and her mother, Linda, drove her home in what Brianne describes as a "piercing silence." With the clouds in her head so dark she believed she would never see light again, Brianne went straight for the bathroom and swallowed every Tylenol and Advil she could find—a total of 74 pills. She was only 14, and she wanted to die.

A few hours later Linda Camilleri found her daughter vomiting all over the floor. Brianne was rushed to the hospital, where she convinced a psychiatrist (and even herself) that it had been a one-time impulse. The psychiatrist urged her parents to keep the episode a secret to avoid any stigma. Brianne's father, Alan, shudders when he remembers that advice. "Mental illness is a closet problem in this country, and it's got to come out" he says. With a schizophrenic brother and a cousin who committed suicide, Alan thinks he should have known better. Instead, Brianne's cloud just got darker. After another aborted suicide attempt a few months later, she finally ended up at McLean Hospital in Belmont, Mass., one of the best mental-health facilities in the country. Now, after three years of therapy and antidepressant medication, Brianne, 19, thinks she's on track. A sophomore at James Madison University in Virginia, she's on the dean's list, has a boyfriend and hopes to spend a semester in Australia—a plan that makes her mother nervous, but also proud.

A Depression "Epidemic" Among Children and Teens?

Brianne is one of the lucky ones. Most of the nearly 3 million adolescents struggling with depression never get the help they need because of prejudice about mental illness, inadequate mental-health resources and widespread ignorance about how emotional problems can wreck young lives. The National Institute of Mental Health (NIMH) estimates that 8 percent of adolescents and 2 percent of children (some as young as 4) have symptoms of depression. Scientists also say that early onset of depression in children and teenagers has become increasingly common; some even use the word "epidemic." No one knows whether there are actually more depressed kids today or just greater awareness of the problem, but some researchers think that the stress of a high divorce rate, rising academic expectations and social pressure may be pushing more kids over the edge.

This is a huge change from a decade ago, when many doctors considered depression strictly an adult disease. Teenage irritability and rebelliousness was "just a phase" kids would outgrow. But scientists now believe that if this behavior is chronic, it may signal serious problems. New brain research is also beginning to explain why teenagers may be particularly vulnerable to mood disorders. Psychiatrists who treat adolescents say parents should seek help if they notice a troubling change in eating, sleeping, grades or social life that lasts more than a few weeks. And public awareness of the need for help does seem to be increasing. One case in point: HBO's hit series "The Sopranos." In a recent episode, college student Meadow Soprano saw a therapist who recommended antidepressants to help her work through her feelings after the murder of her former boyfriend.

Without treatment, depressed adolescents are at high risk for school failure, social isolation, promiscuity, "self-medication" with drugs or alcohol, and suicide—now the third leading cause of death among 10- to 24-year-olds. "The earlier the onset, the more people tend to fall away developmentally from their peers," says Dr. David Brent, professor of child psychiatry at the University of Pittsburgh. "If you become depressed at 25, chances are you've already completed your education and you have more resources and coping skills. If it happens at 11, there's still a lot you need to learn, and you may never learn it." Early untreated depression also increases a youngster's chance of developing more severe depression as an adult as well as bipolar disease and personality disorders.

For kids who do get help, like Brianne, the prognosis is increasingly hopeful. Both antidepressant medication and cognitive-behavior therapy (talk therapy that helps patients identify and deal with sources of stress) have enabled many teenagers to focus on school and resume their lives. And more effective treatment may be available in the next few years. The NIMH recently launched a major 12-city initiative called the Treatment for Adolescents With Depression Study to help determine which regimens—Prozac, talk therapy or some combination—work best on 12- to 18-year-olds.

Brent is conducting another NIMH study looking at newer medications, including Effexor and Paxil, that may help kids whose depression is resistant to Prozac. He is trying to identify genetic markers that indicate which patients are likely to respond to particular drugs.

Doctors hope that the new research will ultimately result in specific guidelines for adolescents, since there's not much evidence about the effects of the long-term use of these medications on developing brains. Most antidepressants are not approved by the FDA for children under 18, although doctors routinely prescribe these medications to their young patients. (This practice, called "off-label" use, is not uncommon for many illnesses.) Many of the drugs being tested—like Prozac and Paxil—are known as SSRIs, or selective serotonin reuptake inhibitors. They regulate how the brain uses the neurotransmitter serotonin, which has been connected to mood disorders.

Identifying Kids at Risk Is Hard

Outside the lab, the hardest task may be pinpointing kids at risk. Depressed teens usually suffer for years before they are identified, and fewer than one in five who needs treatment gets it. "Parents often think their kid is just being a kid, that all teens are moody, oppositional and irritable all the time," says Madelyne Gould, a professor of child psychiatry at Columbia University. In fact, she says, the typical teenager should be more like "Happy Days" than "Rebel Without a Cause." Even adults who make a career of working with kids—teachers, coaches and pediatricians—can misread symptoms. On college campuses, experts say, cases of depression are too often misdiagnosed as mononucleosis or chronic-fatigue syndrome. That's why many kids still suffer unnoticed, even though more schools are using screening tools that identify kids who should be referred for a professional evaluation. Often it's only the overt troublemakers—disruptive or violent kids—who get any attention. "In most cases, if a child is doing adequately in school, is getting decent grades, but seems a little depressed, there's a great likelihood that the child won't come to the attention of the teacher, counselor, administrator or school psychologist," says Phil Lazarus, who runs the school-psychology training program at Florida International University and is chairman of the National Association of School Psychologists' emergency-response team.

And finding the right help can be as difficult as identifying the kids who need help. There are currently only about 7,000 child and adolescent psychiatrists around the country, far fewer than most mental-health experts say is required. The shortage is most acute in low-income areas and there are severe consequences in communities with more than enough traumatic circumstances to trigger a major depression. At the age of 13, Jonathan Haynes of San Antonio was clearly on a dangerous path. His parents, both crack addicts, were homeless—a major risk factor for depression. Haynes did what he says was necessary to survive: sold crack himself, and broke into houses and cars. But his life began to improve in the most unlikely place: jail. In 1999, his parents, by then drug-free, encouraged him to get help. Still high from the marijuana he had smoked that day, Haynes turned himself in to police. At Southton, the county's maximum-security facility for juveniles, he was diagnosed and prescribed antidepressants. Now 18, Haynes works as a cook and lives with his family on San Antonio's East Side. "I got my priorities straight," he says. "I gotta stay strong. I got strong parents. That helps. Ever since I got out of Southton, I've been off the streets."

Several Factors Can Trigger Depression

In his case, it seems clear that traumatic family events contributed to his illness. But more often the trigger for adolescent depression is not so obvious. Scientists are studying a combination of factors, both internal and external. The hormonal surges of puberty have long been shown to affect moods, but now new research says that changes in brain structure may also play a role. During adolescence, the brain's gray matter is gradually "pruned" and unused brain-cell connections are cleared out, creating superhighways that allow us as adults to focus and learn things more deeply, says Dr. Harold Koplewicz, author of "More Than Moody: Recognizing and Treating Adolescent Depression." The link between this brain activity and depression isn't clear, but Koplewicz says the pruning happens between the ages of 14 and 17, when rates of psychiatric disorders increase significantly.

Scientists also believe that there's a genetic predisposition to depression. "The closer your connection to a depressed family member—a depressed father rather than a depressed uncle, for example—the greater an individual's likelihood of suffering depression," says John Mann, chief of the department of neuroscience at Columbia University. Negative experiences, such as growing up in an abusive home or witnessing violence, increases the probability of a depressive episode in kids who are at risk. Doctors around the country reported an influx of young patients after last year's [2001] terrorist attacks, although it's too soon to tell whether this will translate into significantly higher numbers of youngsters diagnosed with major depression. Lisa Meier, a clinical psychologist in Rockville, Md., a Washington, D.C., suburb, says the attacks made many kids' worst fears seem all too real. "Prior to September 11, if a child said they were afraid a bomb would drop on their house, that was very clinically significant, because it was an atypical fear," Meier says. "It's not atypical anymore."

Many depressed adolescents have a long history of trouble, which often includes misdiagnosis and a lot of trial-and-error therapy that can aggravate the social and emotional problems caused by the depression. Morgan Willenbring, 17, of St. Paul, Minn., has suffered from depression since he was 8, but school officials first thought he had attention-deficit disorder. "I think that's because they see that a lot," says his mother, Kate Meyers. "They tend to lump together what they see as acting-out behavior." It took more than two years to figure out a good treatment regimen. Desipramine, one of the older antidepressants, didn't work. Then Willenbring spent six years on Wellbutrin, which was effective but problematical because he needed to take it three times a day. "It's very easy to forget, which was not helping," he says. When he missed too many doses, he had trouble concentrating and got into fights at home. But a month ago he switched to a once-a-day drug called Celexa and says he's doing better. He even managed to get through breaking up with his longtime girlfriend without missing a day of school.

Therapy and Drugs Help Some, but Not All, Patients

The results of the NIMH study may help make life easier for youngsters like Willenbring. The lead researcher, Dr. John March, a professor of child psychiatry at Duke University, says there is already evidence from other studies supporting short-term behavioral therapy and drugs like Prozac and Paxil. But that regimen works only in about 60 percent of cases, and almost half of those patients relapse within a year of stopping treatment. "We're hoping [the study] will tell us which treatment is best for each set of symptoms," March says, "and whether the severity of symptoms biases you toward one treatment or another."

Until the results of that study and others are in, parents and teenagers have to weigh the risk of medication against the very real dangers of ignoring the illness. A recent report from the Centers for Disease Control found that 19 percent of high-school students had suicidal thoughts and more than 2 million of them actually began planning to take their own lives. One of them was Gabrielle Cryan. In 1999, during her junior year at a New York City high school, "I obsessed about death," she says. "I talked about it with everyone." With her parents' help, she found a therapist just before the start of her senior year who "put a name to what I'd been feeling," says Cryan. "My therapist made me realize it, face it and get over it." She also received a prescription for Prozac. Although she had some hesitations about Prozac, "it really did help me," she says. So did the talk therapy. "The first part of the healing process—and I know this sounds corny—was becoming more self-aware," she says. The therapy helped her see that "everything was not a black-and-white situation." Before therapy, little things would throw her into a funk. "I couldn't find my shoe and the whole week was ruined," she says now with a laugh. "They taught me to get some perspective" And while her depression now is "nonexistent," she knows that she may have to face it again in the future. "We're all a work in progress," Cryan says. "But I've picked up a lot of tools. When I feel symptoms coming on, I can reach out and help myself now." Stories like hers are the successes that lead others out of the darkness.

For Further Discussion

1. In Chapter 2 critics are divided on the severity of Holden Caulfield's depression and what has caused it. Some, such as Harrison Smith and Peter Shaw, see him as an unusually sensitive teenager dealing with the normal problems of adolescence. Others, including Ihab Hassan and Peter J. Seng, see Holden's dilemma as the problem of retaining the innocence of childhood while accepting the responsibilities of an adult world. And other critics, such as Duane Edwards and James Bryan, contend that he has significant issues due to unresolved sexual conflicts. Which writer or writers do you most agree with? Why?

2. Robert Coles recounts an interview with noted child psychoanalyst Anna Freud, who tells him that she read *The Catcher in the Rye* after many of her young patients told her they identified with Holden Caulfield. She says she asked these patients, "Tell me what Holden wants me to know!" What does Holden "want us to know"? Why do you think *The Catcher in the Rye* speaks so strongly to adolescents dealing with depression?

3. Joanne Irving finds that Holden Caulfield has high goals of superiority coupled with excessive feelings of inferiority. Do you agree with Irving? What evidence of these goals and feelings do you see in the text of *The Catcher in the Rye*? Why would this combination make someone depressed?

4. Ellen McGrath writes that teenage boys often have difficulty discussing their feelings and that this can be a risk factor for depression. In your opinion, why is communication important? Do you think open discussions about feelings can reduce the effects of depression?

For Further Reading

Robert Cormier, *The Chocolate War*. New York: Pantheon Books, 1974.

William Golding, *Lord of the Flies*. London: Faber & Faber, 1954.

Carol Goodman, *The Lake of Dead Languages*. New York: Ballantine Books, 2002.

Judith Guest, *Ordinary People*. New York: Viking Press, 1976.

Ken Kesey, *One Flew Over the Cuckoo's Nest*. New York: Viking Press, 1962.

John Knowles, *A Separate Peace*. London: Secker & Warburg, 1959; New York: Macmillan, 1960.

Sylvia Plath, *The Bell Jar*. London: Heinemann, 1963.

J.D. Salinger, *Franny and Zooey*. Boston: Little, Brown, 1961; London: Heinemann, 1962.

J.D. Salinger, *Nine Stories*. Boston: Little, Brown, 1953.

J.D. Salinger, *Raise High the Roof Beam, Carpenters and Seymour: An Introduction*. Boston: Little, Brown, 1963; London: Heinemann, 1963.

Curtis Sittenfeld, *Prep*. New York: Random House, 2005.

Bibliography

Books

William Francis Belcher and James Ward Lee *J.D. Salinger and the Critics.* Belmont, CA: Wadsworth Publishing Co., 1962.

Warren G. French *J.D. Salinger, Revisited.* Boston: Twayne Publishers, 1988.

Marilyn E. Gootman and Pamela Espeland *When a Friend Dies: A Book for Teens About Grieving and Healing.* Rev. Ed. Minneapolis: Free Spirit Publishing, 2005.

Henry Anatole Grunwald, ed. *Salinger: A Critical and Personal Portrait.* New York: Harper & Brothers, 1962.

Frederick L. Gwynn and Joseph L. Blotner *The Fiction of J. D. Salinger.* Pittsburgh: University of Pittsburgh Press, 1958; London: Spearman, 1960.

Kenneth Hamilton *J.D. Salinger: A Critical Essay.* Grand Rapids, MI: Eerdmans, 1967.

Marvin Laser and Norman Fruman, eds. *Studies in J.D. Salinger: Reviews, Essays, and Critiques of "The Catcher in the Rye," and Other Fiction.* New York: Odyssey Press, 1963.

James Lundquist *J.D. Salinger.* New York: F. Ungar Publishing Co., 1979.

Joyce Maynard *At Home in the World: A Memoir.* New York: Picador USA, 1998.

James E. Miller Jr.   *J.D. Salinger.* Minnesota: University of Minnesota Press, 1965.

Sanford Pinsker   *"The Catcher in the Rye": Innocence Under Pressure.* New York: Twayne Publishers, 1993.

Periodicals

Leonard D. Baer and Wilbert M. Gesler   "Reconsidering the Concept of Therapeutic Landscapes in J. D. Salinger's *The Catcher in the Rye*." *Area* 36, no. 4 (December 2004): 404–13.

Philip H. Brifithis   "J.D. Salinger and the Psychiatrist." *West Virginia University Philological Papers* 21 (1974): 67–77.

Matt Evertson   "Love, Loss, and Growing Up in J.D. Salinger and Cormac McCarthy." In *"The Catcher in the Rye": New Essays,* edited by J.P. Steed. New York: Peter Lang, 2002.

Vanessa E. Ford   "Coming Out as Lesbian or Gay: A Potential Precipitant of Crisis in Adolescence." *Journal of Human Behavior in the Social Environment* 8, no. 2/3 (June 28, 2004): 93–110.

Ernest Havemann   "The Search for the Mysterious J.D. Salinger: The Recluse in the Rye." *Life*, November 3, 1961.

R. John Huber
and Gail
Ledbetter
"Holden Caulfield, Self-Appointed Catcher in the Rye: Some Additional Thoughts." *Journal of Individual Psychology* 33, no. 2 (November 1977): 250–256.

Jonathan P. Lewis
"All That David Copperfield Kind of Crap: Holden Caulfield's Rejection of Grand Narratives." *Notes on Contemporary Literature* 32, no. 4 (September 2002): 3–5.

Arthur Mizener
"The Love Song of J.D. Salinger." *Harper's Magazine*, February 1959: 83–90.

Charles D. Peavy
"'Did You Ever Have a Sister?': Holden, Quentin, and Sexual Innocence." *Florida Quarterly* 1, no. 3 (1968): 82–95.

John Pilkington
"About This Madman Stuff (Sanity in *Catcher, Huck Finn*)." *Studies in English* 7 (1966): 65–75.

Irene T. Paz Pruitt
"Family Treatment Approaches for Depression in Adolescent Males." *American Journal of Family Therapy* 35, no. 1 (January-February 2007): 69–81.

Ron Rosenbaum
"The Haunted Life of J.D. Salinger." *Esquire,* June 1997.

Mary Suzanne
Schriber
"Holden Caulfield, C'est Moi." In *Critical Essays on Salinger's "The Catcher in the Rye"*, edited by Joel Salzberg. Boston: G.K. Hall, 1990.

John Skow   "Sonny: An Introduction." *Time*, September 15, 1961: 84–90.

Yasuhiro Takeuchi   "The Burning Carousel and the Carnivalesque: Subversion and Transcendence at the Close of *The Catcher in the Rye*." *Studies in the Novel* 34, no. 3 (Fall 2002): 320–36.

Index

CPSIA information can be obtained
at www.ICGtesting.com
Printed in the USA
FFOW02n1902130614
5907FF